STARVING TO LIVE

I SHALL BE, I MUST, I WILL!

BY MICHAEL ANTHONY EPPS

xulon PRESS

Copyright © 2003 by Michael Anthony Epps

Starving to Live
by Michael Anthony Epps

Printed in the United States of America

ISBN 1-591609-72-0

All rights reserved. No part of this book may be reproduced, stored in a retrieval system, or transmitted by any means, electronically, mechanically, photocopying, recording or otherwise without written consent from author.

Unless otherwise indicated, Bible quotations are taken from the King James and Amplified Version of the Bible. Copyright © 1965, 1987 by Zondervan Corporation.

Xulon Press
www.XulonPress.com

Xulon Press books are available in bookstores everywhere, and on the Web at www.XulonPress.com.

God Bless
Yall!!!

Sheldon Epps

ACKNOWLEDGEMENT

First and foremost, I would like to thank God for entrusting me with the gift of beautiful thoughts and visions, and the ability to transfer those thoughts and visions into words. Most of all, I would like to thank Him for his miraculous healing power.

Thanks to those few people who gave a continuous listening ear of support during my days of pregnancy and delivery with this book. David Word, Eric Knott, Pamela Watts, Vivian Thatch-Jackson, and Evangelist Glenn Tate-Bibbs. I thank these wonderful people for their many days of support and encouragement.

Thanks to my brothers in Christ, the soldiers at war who have labored side by side with me throughout this journey. Reggie Cyrus, Leo Davis, Rev. Jesse Branch, and Pastor Dallas C. Wilson. Thanks to these great men of God.

Thanks to my children, who are a very dear part of my life. On many days it was the vision of them that made me determined to press on to be all that I could be, that they would have the best life possible. I love my kids: Rakeem, Ashleigh, Kahlil, and Ni'gere. You are gifts to my life.

To my mother Sandy Hendricks and the rest of my wonderful family, I thank you for the many seeds that you've sown into my life. Thanks for being you.

Last but definitely not least, I thank my warrior princess; my wife Toyena Epps, who pressed, labored, and remained by my side through hell and high waters. I thank her for not giving up on me when most people thought I was crazy. Many people would have run, but this soldier stood firm in wifely love and Godly faith to believe in the vision God has given me. She is one tough cookie. I love you very much.

In closing, I would like to thank the many readers who will read this book. It is because of my belief that there are many people out there who are "Starving to Live" that motivated me to deliver this book. Thank you all for your support.

TABLE OF CONTENTS

CHAPTER ONE - THE WILDERNESS 15
   The Light Beyond the Mountain 17
   Physical Sickness Couldn't Change
      Spiritual Destiny..21
   External Doubt, Internal Hope 25
   Another Day In the Desert 27
   Just Enough Light to Write 29
   Light In the Dungeon 33

CHAPTER TWO - NOT ANOTHER DAY...................35
   Buried Alive 37
   Ordinary? Out of the Question 39
   Smiling Through Pain 43
   Are You Tired Yet?..45
   Prayer For Purpose 49
   Life Behind the Wall 53

CHAPTER THREE - IT BELONGS TO YOU 55
   What's Your Drink?.......................................57
   Are People Suppose to Understand?..............59
   Be True to Your Gift......................................61
   The Light of Truth 63
   Purpose and Grace..67
   The Rain 71

CHAPTER FOUR - LIVE I SAY! 75
The Contractions Are Getting Stronger 77
The Blessing of Purpose.........79
The Memory of You 81
Unspoken Identity 83
The World's Blueprint 85
The Walk - The Reward 89
Breathe! 91
The Sacrifice 95

CHAPTER FIVE - HOW HUNGRY ARE YOU?.........99
The Craving.........101
Don't Keep Hitting the Snooze 105
The Program.........109

CHAPTER SIX - EXCUSES, EXCUSES 113
Sleep Won't Do It.........115
What Are We Waiting For? 117

CHAPTER SEVEN - WHO CARES.........121
Talk Less and Do More 123
The Cocoon Is Ugly, But the Butterfly
  is Beautiful!.........125
The Link 127
The Gambler.........129

CHAPTER EIGHT - THE GIFT.........131
Purpose Is Motivated Without Pay.........133
Gifts Expose God 137
Another Life Form 141

CHAPTER NINE - FIRE FUELS THE FIERCE......145
- Vitamins For Purpose 147
- Fury! 151
- Sorrow 155
- The Wind 159

CHAPTER TEN - LOSE YOURSELF 161
- You're Adding the Wrong Numbers 163
- Free! 165
- The Force...167
- The Boxer and The Fighter 171
- The Fear Factor 175
- Be Encouraged 177

The most sorrowful man is not the man who has no vision and dies. The most sorrowful man is the man who has the vision, but not enough faith to fulfill it.

INTRODUCTION

Here I lay within the shell of this body, as I peek through weakened eyes. My mind is telling me to get up, but my body is refusing to move. Am I dead? What's going on? Somebody tell me something, I'm scared! I can vaguely see members of my family across the room, but how is this possible? Other than my wife, most of my family lives hundreds of miles from here? It would take my mother at least 13 hours to get to Chicago, and I know I haven't been sleep 13 hours. Have I? The last thing I remember, I was in intensive care struggling to breathe. I remember the doctor telling me, he wanted to put me on a machine to help me breathe. Now I wake up in this strange place? Why is everyone looking at me like that? I can see them smiling with their mouths, but their eyes are saying something totally different. Someone get me a mirror, I whisper. Oh no! I've grown a full beard and lost almost 40 pounds. How can you grow a full beard in a day? I whisper to my wife, "what day is this?" She says, Saturday. Saturday, I'm thinking? Saturday!!! The last time I was conscious, it was Sunday. Now it's Saturday! That's not possible, unless...oh God! I've been sleep a week! That's crazy! No, what's crazy is my wife says it's been "two weeks." Nearly two weeks in a coma, that's how long I've been on the other side. And now I've awakened downtown in the hospital. My wife tells me I was flown here by helicopter. I always wanted to tour the city by helicopter, but not like this. My family and friends have been praying for my awakening, and now it's here. So this is my reality, one day I'm in my garage working, I come in contact with some infected wood, in and out of the hospital for 4 months, and now I'm waking up from a coma. This is crazy. So, now what, "Am I going to die?" I can't die; I'm only 37 years old. God, can you hear me! I want to live! Please God, I want to live!

The funny thing about life is you don't realize how important it is until it's almost taken. It's amazing how we know we have been called to do certain things, but we keep putting them off. We truly believe we will have tomorrow to accomplish them, and then you possibly wake up one day like me, if you wake up? The sad thing is that if we are to leave this world right this moment, what have we done? What mark have we left behind that we'll be remembered by? In a whole life span, how did we live? It's no secret, we all have those internal visions and dreams that we should be fulfilling, but fear, yes I said fear, is robbing you of your fulfillment. As a result, you may one day find that it's too late. As for me, "All Glory be to God" that it's now one year later, as I sit here healed from the sickness writing this book. I got another chance to fulfill my purpose, and believe me; I am not stopping for anything or anybody! I never thought I would be saying this, but my near death experience was the best thing that happened to me. It thrust me into my purpose, and gave me life. I now know what faith truly is, and I am determined to live fulfilled. I refuse to live another day in survival mode, just getting by! I am determined to now live victorious through the power of God, and get what's mine!

So, now I come to you with the power of determination to reach out, and share what I know. If there's something that you know you have been called to do, don't hesitate!

Starving to Live

The time is now! If you can feel the ache in your soul, and the fire in your spirit to reach for something greater, then "Starving To Live" is your book. I promise you, you won't be disappointed. Through faith I have step out beyond the norm to apprehend that which I was "chosen" to do. I now challenge you to do the same. God has placed something unique within you, which not only describes you, but is you! Are you hungry? Are you starving for something greater for your life? Then, "Starving To Live" is for you! Don't accept the lie that great things only happen to certain people. I am living proof that there is something great within each of us. "Starving to Live" will show you that the only difference between successful purpose fulfilled people and those unfulfilled is our willingness and determination.

I present to you my powerful purpose filled brothers and sisters, "Starving to Live." You Shall Be! You Must! You Will! May you be empowered to live!

CHAPTER 1

THE WILDERNESS

YOU CAN OFTEN SEE BETTER IN THE DARK!

The Light Beyond The Mountain

We don't always understand why we have to take certain journeys in our life, be it to cities, states or countries. We are drawn to travel beyond the mountain of our routine and ordinary path to the great beyond. I have found that these journeys aren't always to get us to a destination, but rather to get us to destiny. They aren't always to get us to a place, but to deliver us to purpose. Whether these trips are taken consciously or unconsciously, in the sense of us not actually knowing why we are led to go to a particular place, often these moves become the most essential piece to the puzzle of purpose. There have been many great people in history that started out just ordinary people at the beginning of their journey. However, as they pressed on to get to their destination, their lives and the lives of others were changed forever.

In today's time, we see on television professionals of all sort; actors, actresses, musicians, and athletes who journeyed beyond the valley of limitation and found unknown treasures waiting. Many of these people that we see were just local favorites, but once they journeyed beyond the mountains, they were embraced on the world's stage.

In these missions many have met and found people and things that would change their lives and the lives of others forever. In fact, many have even journeyed to meet their mates for life in the most unusual places. From the moment their paths crossed, they knew with great internal truth it was destiny. Often the journey can happen through a job, a vacation or simply a magnetic pull to a certain place, and there we begin our greatest fulfillment towards purpose.

I remember when I got out of the military back in 1992, at Fort Bragg, N.C. after 7 years of duty. I thought about moving back North, because New Jersey had played an important part in helping to insert several pieces to the puzzle of my life. However, many people spoke of Atlanta, Georgia as being a truly favorable move, it was considered the southern land of opportunity. Now that I was a civilian, my greatest concern was to get somewhere and start working. So with great faith I went to Georgia, a place I had never been, to find what belonged to me. I can thankfully say I found a job awaiting me the first day I went looking for work. It was a job working on Ft. McPherson Army base as a barber. However, this would in no way be my most memorable reality of Georgia. What became my most blinding reality was the intense call to the ministry and the man who would help me along the way. His name was Pastor Dallas C. Wilson, of the Center of Hope Church Of God In Christ. Pastor Wilson was positioned to embrace me and help me along this journey into the ministry. I am not saying that God couldn't have called me anywhere else, but it was the amazing provisions that he made for me from the moment I arrived in Atlanta. In the beginning, I wasn't clear as to why I had come to Atlanta. However, one of the greatest gifts that I would ever received, was being unlocked. This was all happening in a place that I had never thought of going, and everything was already in position. My second day in Atlanta I met Pastor Wilson and his choir while they were during a street concert. This was their first and only concert to my knowledge during that time. I thought it was by coincidence that our paths crossed, but this man played an important part in my life. He provided me with a place to stay in his home, food to eat, and a brotherly relationship that we have maintained to this very day. I truly believe Pastor Dallas was there for the purpose of receiving me at that part of my journey, even though I was a total stranger to him. It's funny now, as I look back, how the course seemed to have been supernaturally mapped out.

About three years later, while working at the army base, I met a friend by the name of Demetrius Robinson who would play a major part in the next part of my journey. Demetrius and I had been friends for about eight months, when he asked me to ride with him home to Chicago to see his family before he was shipped off to Korea. At first, I wasn't really interested, mainly because I was an eastern boy. Outside of Oprah and Michael Jordan, I didn't really know too much about Chicago, but I said, "cool." The night we arrived in Chicago, we went downtown to hang out on the beach at Lake Michigan. I remember having this funny feeling while I was out there. I remember telling Demetrius, how Chicago felt like home, he just smiled. The funny thing is that I hadn't really been anywhere in Chicago, neither had I done anything there, but I just felt this reality. The next day we went out to eat and enjoy the town; Chi-town that is. While at a restaurant, I met a young lady; little did I know that our meeting would change my life forever. I remember having just gone through a bad relationship about eight months earlier, so a relationship was the last thing on my mind. However, that wouldn't matter because here after two days in Chicago, I now stood face to face with my future wife. Yes, I said wife, Miss Toyena Shamberger, who would shortly become my better half. She told me later that she knew the moment we met that we would be together. I on the other hand, wasn't trying to listen to what I knew within. By the third day it became inevitable that I was to see her again, so I called her for a date. As a result of this second meeting, I knew with a deep internal confirmation what was destined to happen. To make an amazingly long story short, within two months I was relocated and married. I can truly say, that God has continuously blessed us. In regards to Demetrius, the week after he and I returned to Atlanta, he was relocated to Korea; I have never seen him since. I strongly believe it was purposed that we met, that we journeyed together and that I was delivered to my destination.

My life has consisted of me living in 6 states and 2 countries. Believe me each has played an important role in my overall development. I have always been willing or as some may say, "crazy enough to journey beyond the mountains of the known, to discover the unknown part of purpose that awaited. I am not saying to just get up and take off, but if you see the light beyond the mountain, maybe it's trying to lead you to your destiny. Can you afford not to take the journey?

Physical Sickness Couldn't Change Spiritual Destiny

In November 2001 my life was greatly changed, as I faced one of the most challenging and devastating times in my life. I acquired an almost incurable virus called blastomycosis, from some infected wood while working in my garage. As a result, I was in and out of the hospital for 4 straight months, almost dying on two occasions. However, because of the wonderful miraculous power of God and prayer, I was finally able to reclaim a life at home in April of 2002. I remember before this life changing experience happened, I had started writing notes for my first book "A Hunger To Behold" back in late August of 2001. At that time, little did I know that my life would take a turn that would greatly change me forever? For six months, my life and everything in it came to a screeching halt: my family, my job and my purpose as I fought for my life. One day while sitting at home and reflecting, I remember feeling more than justified mentally, emotionally and spiritually to do nothing other than mope.

I remember looking across the room and seeing the "notebook" which I thought held the power to possibly change the destiny of my life and my family's as well.

Unfortunately, it seemed as though it had been an eternity since I had picked up a pen or even read any of the stuff I had written. Therefore, as for me being a writer, it seems to be a just crazy idea of the past, so I thought. For the next few weeks, I did all I could to ignore "the notebook." You see, the sickness, the mental struggles from almost losing my life, and the fact that I now couldn't even walk, had all beaten me to a pulp. However, one day while lying on the couch in pity and misery, I heard an internal voice telling me to get up and get my notebook. Now here was not only a mental challenge, but a physical challenge as well, being that I had been immobile for many months. I was now convinced that I didn't have the strength in anyway to get to neither that notebook nor whether I even wanted to get up to get it. But, one thing that I found out was that this voice was not going to go away. Though I would continuously ignore it, it would come back again and again. After a period of time, I was walking through the house with the help of my walker when I heard the voice again, this time louder than ever. Something inside of me was now demanding that I go and get the notebook! So finally I did. To my amazement as I read some of my notes, I found out that even though I had physically been beaten to smithereens, deep within me my purpose was still alive. Best of all, as I continued to read my notes, I became empowered once again with purpose, vision, and fulfillment. In fact, it was because of me grabbing hold to my powerful purpose that helped me to rise from the grave of my depression and frustration. The sickness had only blinded me: wedging a barrier between my destined purpose and me. But the moment I was exposed back to it's truth, it once again led me to see the real me; the purpose filled man that God had destined for great things. Amazingly enough, after having experienced all that I experienced, I had the audacity to not only finish the greatly inspired book, "A Hunger To Behold," but to also begin writing this blessed book. Through all this I gained a powerful understanding about purpose; that though it may be carried out in the physical, it's not born in the physical. And though we may become physical hindered, purpose because of its power waits patiently, at least for a while. I have come to realize that even when I couldn't walk, couldn't talk or recognize its existence: Purpose was still alive and waiting. I proclaim to you therefore, that physical sickness couldn't change spiritual destiny.

External Doubt, Internal Hope

King David wrote in Psalms chapter 27, verse 13, " I had fainted, unless I had believed to see the goodness of the Lord in the land of the living." In other words, when the heaviness of our burdens are weighing us down and the tidal waves of our circumstances try to knock us off our feet; when all seems lost and our bodies are tired and weary, we should faint, but there is a light deep within us. In fact, this beacon of light is a direct message relay system that receives messages of spiritual empowerment directly from God. It is his way of telling us to hold on to our belief, for change is coming. These infused jolts of hope push us a few steps farther as they revive us from the suffocation of daily living, as life's challenges try to smother us. This hope is not fleshly related, due to the fact that the flesh is distracted by the perception of gathered information from the external world. This hope is spiritually related, infused by God into our spirits that we would be who we are, based on who He sees us as. This spiritually crazy hope overrides what the body is struggling with, what it hears the mind wrestling with and anything else that tries to distract us. It's a power of spiritual authority that keeps us standing, even when we could have, would have or should have fainted. Like soldiers carrying casualties on a torn battle field of war to safety, this spiritually empowerment positions itself within us in a rescue position and carries or even drags us to safety. If for but a moment our internal hope carries us away from the rapid explosions of life, that we would be able to find peace and patience in the reality of the greater days ahead.

However, because our hope is often seeded so deeply, it's not until we reach a state of physical overload that we realize it's there. Unfortunately, by this time we often have reached a point where we are struggling to believe and unable to go on, as we gasp for air within the valley of despair. Fortunately, hope tells us to take a breath and see the light beckoning just beyond the hill. It tells us to hear the flow of the quenching waters just up ahead, as it relays the message from home base telling us to walk just a little farther for provisions and abundance are waiting. Most Importantly, no matter how tired or distraught we may get, we must let hope carry us to the refuge of fulfillment. Hope is the internal confirmation of the unseen, in contrast to the frustrations of what is seen. Internal hope can be a powerful resuscitator in our daily lives as we journey to reach our destiny.

Another Day In The Desert

Here we are facing another day, in which we must stand in the hot scorching reality of where we are. We're running low on endurance, almost out of oxygen, as we suffocate from the humidity of unfulfillment. We try to be optimistic as we look around, but unfortunately for miles things seem the same. Can we take another step, and if we did would we sadly find the same thing? It seems we have walked for many miles over the years just to find that our present location resembles our past reality. Now we stand starving to fulfill the empty ache of our soul as we individually ask ourselves the question, " Can I accomplish something that seems to be such a great feat, when it seems to be only me standing out here all alone?" How do we cross the mountain of past failures, in the present heat of reality, through the wilderness of the uncertainty? It seems that we have been in this land alone for so long, wrapped only in our desire for fulfillment. In fact, by now we should have fainted; if not for the voice of reality within which keeps us company, while demanding that we go on. Amazingly enough, though this voice is within us, we seem to also hear it up ahead in the distance telling us to come, for fulfillment is near. As a result, on some days we crawl, other days we walk, there are even those days after a good night's sleep that we awake running. Because of this, I am now convinced that the race is not always given to the strongest runner, or to the thinker, but it is given to the one with the enduring belief that he can and will finish. For those of you who are reading this, the desert can symbolize whatever seemingly endless everyday reality that you cross in trying to fulfill your purpose and dreams. These realities can seem blazingly brutal to that which we know we are destined to do. They can literally make us feel as if we are isolated in an uninhabited land; standing there by ourselves with no one to understand this journey which we have been called to fulfill. A moment ago, I expressed the reality of the voice that is within us, which also seems to at times lead us from a distance as well. It is important to point out that both voices are one. The inward voice is the voice of purpose, our internal existence that speaks from within to the natural man revealing its existence. The distant pulling voice is the voice of God speaking to us, demanding that we press on to fulfill our destined purpose. You will notice that whether we are in a crowd or alone, the voice becomes evident as needed. In fact, when we are alone it can bring greater clarity to our understanding. If we will listen, it has the ability to give direction, insight, and can create within us a picture or vision that will eventually become an external reality. Our desert days can be long and hard at times, but if we remain true to that which is within, we will be led to the river of fulfillment. Let purpose be your guide!

Just Enough Light

In those dark and uncertain moments of our lives, when we aren't sure which direction to go, purpose can become the breath of light that we need to lead the way. During these flustering moments, purpose can become our air supply and beacon of internal strength. Purpose is a force of internal light that refuses not to shine, even when we are congested by external weights of distraction. Purpose digs through and tears down any and everything that tries to conceal it. Unlike the element of hope or desire, purpose is fiercely more powerful. To be a little more precise, when we hope for something, it is the mere reality of a wishful expectation toward something with a pushing possibility that maybe it will come to pass. We recognize its existence, we hold strongly towards its manifestation, but fulfillment is only found in the apprehension of that which we are hoping for. As well, the power and fulfillment of a desire, rests solely in the reality of its actual manifestation in our life. Neither of these have any true power unless that which they are aiming at is obtained. Now you could probably say there's a thin line dividing the three, based on how they've been defined mentally and emotionally. However, the true difference between the three is that purpose is purely spiritual. It is that which God has placed within us, which is not merely part of us, but is us. Purpose is defined truly by the power of its existence; meaning that regardless of how we feel or how we think, it exists as an unwavering truth that often defines us. Purpose has the power to create a 50-foot tree from an unseen seed, and it can be an ear shattering reality heard only by its possessor. I often think of how life just doesn't make sense sometimes, as a result, we find ourselves reaching and grabbing, trying to find our way through. It is during these confusing moments, that purpose can become the only clear and precise thing in our lives.

I titled this segment, " Just Enough Light", for one simple reason, in my darkest moments when nothing seemed to make sense, when pieces weren't fitting together, the only light of clarity that I could see was coming from my purpose as a writer. I'm talking about, through being almost fatally sick, to financially overwhelmed, it seemed that each step I took led me deeper into darker territory. However, whenever I stopped wandering, and focused, I could see the light of purpose pulling and guiding me out of that darkness. It was as if purpose had already traveled through the dark stormy wilderness, journeyed ahead to claimed territory and then came back for me. Honestly, things just didn't make sense to me a lot of days. I mean I was so entangled by all that was going on with and around me that I thought the only thing that could save me was something happening externally. Now, my next statement is probably going to cause a pause for some of my readers, maybe even a frown, but there were times during my sickness, financial struggles and mental exhaustion, that I believe to this very day, was part of God's intent. I say this because I had to understand that purpose was not something that could be taken lightly or selfishly. It's a predestined mission and empowerment that will affect our lives and the lives of others. But sometimes because of our fears or immaturity or other distractions, we deny or rebuke our purpose. In other words, we fight against it.

Most Importantly, I believe that just like God placed water, food, and air on this earth for our sustainment, he also placed things within us that are just as much a part of our sustainment as well. However, it is up to us to recognize, embrace and nurture these internal and powerful gifts of life. We must get busy, that our piece to the puzzle of life can be delivered to the needed areas and lives as predestined. Above all, I believe that when we don't nurture or act upon that which God has given, then we find intense struggle, confusion, and stressfulness in life. I believe we are often allowed to experience the darkness that we would see the light.

In addition, I know that God is more than wise enough to empower more than one person to fulfill his purpose, but he injects within us that which he has designed to be a light for our path. Unfortunately, due to our wandering and stubbornness, we spend a life of guessing and re-guessing. I have tried my hands at many things in life and have been pretty good at some, but the one thing that had no external support, justification, or certainty is my most effortless and empowering execution; my purpose as a writer. We can choose not to adhere to the voice within and delay or even literally bury it with us in the grave. But, it is my hope that you will allow the internal light to give you life. You will be surprised that when we stop looking around and look within, we will see just enough light to see our purpose, which will lead us out of our dark despair. Truly, it's often in the dark despair that we are able to see the divinely illuminated light.

Light In The Dungeon

Here we are chained in the dungeon to our failures, mistakes, and hurts. Often times, we seem unable to accomplish the simplest things, as these realities rattle in the dungeon of our soul. Amazingly enough, in this dark place, we still seem able to see light. What does this light mean? Furthermore, in our tired and frustrated state, does this light even matter? Is this light a spiritual reality or a wishful illusion? The difference is that a wishful illusion is a last attempt that we create in our minds, in which we hope something will find us and lead us out of this despair of unfulfillment. We aren't really sure what, but we grab hold to anything that tends to have the ability to free us. On the other hand, spiritual reality, this illuminating light is just that, reality. With great power it pierces through the thick wall of doubt and warms the cold atmosphere of emptiness, telling us that we are not alone nor without power. Unfortunately, it is not until we have failed at everything with our external ability and been secluded inward that we see this light of reality, our internal purpose and ability. This light is so true and so powerful, that with all the justification we have to lay wounded inward, it breaks through revealing to us the greatness of a power we have yet to behold. Best of all, this light is the light of true purpose with a divine nature that has the power to strengthen us the moment we embrace its rays. No matter how long we have laid confused and unsure if we will ever escape who we have been, this light can take the self imprisoned P.O.W. (Prisoner of War) and set us free. It can release us back into the world to begin our life as a purposed filled people without limit. Often, after being locked away in certain realities, the dark bitterness of failure can begin to blind our eyes to any truth outside of what we have seen. However, if we would only be still and envision beyond the mind to see the spirit, it will show us the light. We must understand that real internal truth can't always be externally seen because of the external distractions and movement. Fortunately, that which is internal is enduring, being able to withstand the test of time. This makes it possible in our darkest moment to be able to see this prevailing light. The light in the dungeon is the envisioned reality that there is still hope. If we fail to embrace this inward empowerment, we shall never begin our outward journey of freedom and fulfillment. Above all that we do, we must embrace the light in the dungeon, for it is God's signal to freedom.

Chapter 2

NOT ANOTHER DAY!

NOW IS THE TIME TO FULFILL PURPOSE

Buried Alive

Beneath the soils of this flesh, buried deep within, you feel and hear the calling of true purpose, as it claws and scratches at your soul to be freed. Does the world know that you have committed such a crime as to smother and bury the gift of purpose, which was meant to be a blessing to so many? The funny thing is that we don't see ourselves as criminals, and in a sense we're right, as far as committing an actual crime. Although, a revealing reality shows that criminals do things that alter their lives and the lives of others everyday, and live with it buried deep within them. So the question becomes, Are there poems, songs, paintings, or novels buried within you that you know are illegally hidden in your personal storage? If so, you should know that they were meant to change the lives of many people. These buried gifts have the power to empower, sustain, help and give hope to starving groups of people. Unfortunately, you have choked and buried them alive because of your dilemmas, barriers, and fears! Let's deal strictly with self for a moment. How long have you known of the greater you? With that same thought, how long has the greater you been buried? Do you ever hear that inner you calling, crying or screaming to be free? Do you ever feel it scratching at your skin, begging for relief? Or maybe you find yourself lying awake at night, sad and sorrowful at the reality of how you are living? Is the internal pain causing external misery? These are but a few realities that we face when our "power to be" is buried alive.

By now you might be wondering, how do we uncover the gift, the purpose and the dream? The first step is to embrace the fact that it exists! Don't just think of this internal nagging as just a mere continuous idea. See it in association to who you are: the unseen you and who you want to be. In addition, embrace it to the fullest; meaning, let it guide and lead you. Listen to it as it expresses itself. If it's not afraid to express itself, then don't be afraid to listen and see the beauty of its reality. That which is within you is beautiful and it's beauty is to be shared. Vincent VanGough painted many paintings from the beauty of his soul. To many art lovers these paintings were considered odd and even strange, while others found them to be of the utmost beauty. In fact, many of his paintings now sell for millions of dollars because of their soulful beauty. Now, while most us may not have VanGough's treasure within us, we do have something truly beautiful within our souls to offer. However, we must realize that the beauty of that which is buried within us shouldn't be ignored too long. Due to the facts, that like all things with life, it can suffocate and often time dies. Sadly to say, we one day come to realize that we now only have the haunting memories of that which was once alive within us. When will we realize that one of the greatest crimes we can ever commit; is to rob ourselves, our families, our friends and those of the world of the gifts buried alive within us?

Ordinary? Out Of The Question

Think about an ordinary life, living within the norm; that which requires only the basics. If it was mentally up to some of us based on what we've been through in life up to this point, ordinary is easily acceptable. However, even through the cold realities that many of us face, once we have felt the internal blaze of purpose, we can accept nothing less than the total embracing of this divine inferno. There are a lot of us who have lived through many situations where things haven't always been in our favor. Believe me I know! We have let down ourselves, as well as having others let us down. Because of these let downs, it has become hard for some of us to reach past the comfort zone of the norm. These realities have become concrete blocks of justification; keeping some locked in place and roped tightly to mediocrity. Even when the heat of the internal flame is felt, the heavy fear of uncertainty tries to smother this fire or at least keep it to a minimum. Though fear may be a bullying reality; there is a greater reality that we must face, which is that many of us know we were not meant to be ordinary or average. In fact, we undoubtedly know that within us is something special. Whether we share this gift with the world or bury it with us in our grave, ordinary has never been the question. We must also realize if we accept ordinary as reality too long it becomes truth, slowly killing the internal life that breeds within us. Sadly, we begin to justify what we see instead of what we know, as ordinary sight begins to make more sense than spiritual reality. It is important that we come to realize that God made each of us unique and that he gave us a greater mission than simply occupying planetary space. He placed a divine purpose in each of us when we were created that defines us as special. Often times the problem is a result of us not fully being taught this, therefore we don't realize what we actually possess. We are traditionally pushed to grab hold of the first thing that will help us reach maximum external accumulation, while burying the true treasure inside. Now don't get me wrong, by me being a family man, I fully understand the need for wanting family to have the best. Therefore finding the best job has always been important to me. But, I also realized that in trying to meet society's definition of what was deemed as living, if I wasn't careful I could have been drawn into a rigorous external mission. This mission would lead me totally away from internal truth and purpose. It's no secret that we live our lives surrounded by the vividly sketched social definition of extraordinary. As a result, we reach and grab at any ladder near us in hope of climbing to the top of the highest structure that will bring us acceptable status. The funny thing is when we get there we find ourselves to be just another part of the worker ant group trying to survive. Yes, we may have a few more things than before, yet we are still ordinary in the measurement of internal purpose. We must come to realize that we cannot grab at just anything in an attempt to be somebody. While we work in the realm of someone else's fulfillment with a few external accolades, we become irritated and aggravated in our own uniqueness. Time has proven to have a way of diluting the external accumulations to expose the internal unfulfillment.

    I remember my first year in Chicago, my mother-in-law knew of a man who was looking for an assistant in his company downtown. She introduced me to him and eventually I got the job. Now the funny thing is, I always wanted to work for a large corporation, having my own office, phone, etc. So, I had finally arrived! I remember in the beginning it was unbelievable to have all of this, and how I thought I had the chance to make a difference. However, reality came the moment I began to try to express creativity. Let's just say, that's not what I was hired for. Sadly to say, within me laid abundant life, yet nowhere to release it. Though I made good money, my daily life remained the same, ordinary and limited. I remember sitting in my office day after day, feeling as though I was dying on the inside. As a result, the bottled up flame inside me began to affect my attitude and disposition. Some of you may probably say I was crazy; I had the metro, the office, and the money. I say who cares, because being alive in every aspect of the word is more important than just having stuff. Well, eventually my disposition was noticed and I was later set free (smile). No regrets!

What I am saying is that even with money, to be ordinary was out of the question. Now I will express that money can sometimes help you get to where you are truly trying to go, as long as you remain true to purpose and don't let the acquiring of money blind you. To make money and meet the social measurements of life is O.K. too. But you must ask yourself, are you fulfilling that which you were born to do, that which makes you unique and special? If you are, great! If not, then don't be surprised to wake up one day with all your stuff, just to find out that you've lived in an external masquerade of your true internal purpose. The bible says, "What does it profit a man to gain the entire world and lose his soul?" Ordinary? You answer the question!

Smiling Through Pain

Be it when you wake up in the morning or while going through your daily activity, you may find yourself laughing at the painful reality of the internal hurt of unfulfillment. I have seen how we put on "the face", smiling with that cheese-eating grin, as we perpetrate the fraud: masquerading our internal unhappiness. Have you ever hated a job so much that you found yourself habitually speaking under your breath, behind that painful smile you constantly presented? Maybe even to keep from alarming or disappointing a love one you continued to smile each morning, as you faced another day at company X. Unfortunately, each day that we refuse to embrace the reality that we are not just another number on the assembly line of life, we wound the internal being of purpose, which wants to live. A perfect example of this is: have you ever had a major disagreement with a love one prior to going to work? All the way to work in the car and right up to the front door, the pain got greater. As you walked inside to begin your day, you put on "the face", giving your good mornings here and your good mornings there. In reality, the internal pain fiercely reminded you that you wanted or needed to be home dealing with and working this situation out. The key words, "working out." Man, talk about a hard job! Your whole inside is killing you and the only thing you can do is smile. In fact, if your boss told a joke you'd strenuously push out a laugh. Often times we laugh through our pain and nobody knows but us. This can become a daily reality to those who live with unfulfilled purposes. For while we smile and laugh we also hurt and cry. We greatly feel the reality and need to be the people we were born to be. So, as the life of this truth gets stronger and stronger, the misery of unfulfillment gets greater and greater.

    I remember back when I was a teenager, I had the opportunity to help start a city dance group. As I recall the times that we performed, I remember we would be backstage divided about which dance routine to do. A few members and myself wanted to do one routine, while the others wanted to do something else. We would be arguing and debating right up to the moment the call person came to tell us it was time to go on. Fortunately, one of the sides would give in for the sake of performing. By now we were all tense, but I remember going out on stage smiling, while knowing that we were hating the reality of what was happening. We smiled and waved as if nothing had ever happened, while on the inside we were all frustrated and angry. Well, as a result the group eventually broke up; each of us attempting to fulfilled our individual dance quests. I used this story to show that we each hold individual gifts, talents, and journeys that we must fulfill. Until we have given them a chance to manifest, we may find ourselves falsely smiling and laughing on the stage of life. We cannot dilute that which is within us or expect others to always understand our intense need to fulfill it. One thing I know for sure is, when we are not true to that which is within us; it will be true to us in being a painful reminder of unfulfillment.

Are You Tired Yet?

One day while talking with a friend, he began telling of his frustration; of how he was tired from having to drive almost an hour and thirty minutes to and from work each day. Now for some of you, you're probably saying that's a jog in the park compared to the distance that some of you might travel to work. And you are right; it can be relatively short going to or from most metropolitan cities. However, the question that I posed to him was, "was he tired of the drive or was he tired of the job?" You see, it wouldn't really matter if you drove an hour and thirty minutes or whether you simply had to walk a block or two to work. The problem is not the journey, it's the destination. Whether our trip is long or short, some of us know our fate before we arrive at our jobs. We know what to expect, "that same old, same old routine." We know the ritual of the morning scenario by heart; who will be sitting in the snack area, who will arrive early and who will get there late. Unfortunately, our jobs are systematical, part of that universal assembly line. And though we may work under different descriptions, if we were to talk with each other, we would find that the patterns are the same. We fall into our cubicles or offices for those that are fortunate, and begin our verbal sparring with the many callers that we must encounter. In other words, whatever it is that we do; we crank up our motors, follow our daily maps, and veer not to the left, nor to the right. Question, have you ever found yourself preparing your mind mentally, "just to go to work?" You know, going through that mental warm-up exercise as you drive to your job or as you walk through the door. All of these things are not unusual, just like it is not unusual for my friend to feel a burden as he drives to work.

Let me shine some light on a hidden fact; there is a great difference between waking up to a job and waking up to a fulfilling day. There is a great un-seen energy that drives you, if you are going to something fulfilling. This energy launches out of the bed and out of your house like a lottery ticket holder going to receive their prize. It makes you anxious, because you can hardly wait to see what you are going to get for the day. There is an excitement because joyfully you don't know what to expect. However, this energy also has a reverse mode, for if you are not being drawn by internal fulfillment, it can also nail you to the bed. It can make your drive to work seem as if you're walking along the highway after your car has just broken down. This is the energy that can make you start counting the hours, the minutes, and the seconds before you even fully get into the door of your job. The tiredness that is often experienced is the weight of knowing that while you labor within the depths of the coal mine, someone else is experiencing a mountainous experience. They're living out their dream and their purpose to the highest degree, doing what they were meant to do. Each day for them is an opportunity to show those who sit ringside why they wear the title, why they're champion. This is not because they like to fight, but simply because they were born to fight! It's almost as if you knew in your heart, that you were to be a hot dog vendor and own your own cart in the park. I guarantee you that you would wake up each morning, buns steaming and dogs cookin'.

Purpose is often the direct source of our dreams and our dreams are what we call our own. When we fulfill purpose, we don't just fulfill a dream, but we fulfill that claim for self-worth. For we know that which we do is our own. It's our uniqueness and our identity.

As long as we work or operate under the overshadowing purpose of someone else, we will always hate the drive. And though we may get excited on payday, Monday comes quickly, just to remind you. For what lives outside of our heart, doesn't belong to us; and we are soon to get bored, tired and frustrated. Sometimes tired can be good though, because it is often at this point that we make a move or do something about our tiredness. Being tired can be that motivating factor that we need sometimes to say, "somehow I will begin to live, and not die (living humdrum). "I will live and live fulfilled!" My question to you is, "Are you tired yet?"

Prayer For Purpose

Hopefully, by now from reading this book you, have come to accept purpose as a spiritual empowerment. This acceptance should be based on the fact that purpose is not something that's devised in our minds, concocted from our education, nor validated by our external realities. Purpose is by far, a power of spiritual existence, being that it existed before we existed. For as God saw the vision of earth and what was to exist therein, he also saw purpose and the vessels he would use to fulfill it. God saw ideas, needs, and creations through which man would bring forth. God set up a timetable in which we would be introduced to the divine mission, which he placed within all of us. This introduction may come through a course of situations or circumstances that the hidden glow of purpose would burst through within our insight. Best of all, regardless of our position or status in life, the spiritual vault would one day begin to release the reality of who we were meant to be.

As I have often said, there are many people who've had fruitful careers, rowing North in their career boats and suddenly they began to steer hard South. Purpose spoke to them with it's demanding voice of authority; overruling their accomplishments and their status. If you think this to be strange, what about the average guy out there trying to make ends meet, who one day decides to drop everything to chase what we may consider an "idea?" Purpose is powerful and in many cases can't be denied as we may witness. But what do we do, when we find ourselves standing face to face with purpose at some point? Well, I have a saying that will help address this particular situation, " if you want to know about a child, then go meet the parents." In other words, go to the roots in which the plant grows. Therefore, if purpose is brewing in your life and it has introduced itself to you, then you now need to get clarity. Find out what direction God wants you to go with it and how to execute its delivery "properly." These questions are very important because many people discover their purpose, but fail to understand it. They often misuse it or even fail to maximize its full potential. This is mainly because purpose in every sense is a "spiritual force," therefore we must get spiritual instructions. In the simplest form of this process, we must learn to listen quietly within ourselves to hear from the source, what it is that we are to do. The most important part of this process is we must converse with the architect of this divine plan, meaning God. Believe me, when you are operating in true purpose, you must stay in constant tune with the spiritual flow of understanding, mainly because purpose will often have to lead us through the wilderness and across the desert to it's place of manifestation. If we are not sure of our direction and instructions, we will find ourselves lost and confused. I'm not saying build a shrine that we enter into with our shoes off. I'm simply saying talk with the "Purpose Giver." Here is a brief prayer that you can try or you can create your own, just make sure it's genuinely from within.

> Father, first and foremost, I would like to thank you for letting me live to see this day and the opportunity to be able to fulfill my purpose.
> Father, I know that you have made me unique,

with a unique mission.

And though I may have wasted a lot of time up to this point, thank you for not giving up on me and that which I am destined to do.

Now that I realize there is a greater purpose for my life, I ask you to help me to understand my purpose.

Help me Father to maximize its use for my life and through my life. I need your wisdom and instructions daily that I may move accordingly.

I know that spiritual things can often conflict with natural things, so whatever and wherever my purpose may lead me, give me the strength to endure and persevere over all obstacles.

And though I may have to stand-alone at times, let the power of it's reality keep me driven.

Father, let the strength of patience have its place in my life that I may not become impatient or doubtful during this journey.

I surrender to you and purpose that the power of your purpose may flow freely through me.

Thank you for where you are taking me. To the Most High and All Seeing God,
In Jesus Name, Amen.

In this prayer I simply ask for understanding, strength, endurance and patience.

Most importantly, I surrendered to the Source and the force of purpose, that it might be maximized through my life. There is no one set prayer; the object is that we find a way to converse with God so that the power of purpose will be accurately released to take flight.

I remember one day while sitting on a plane, waiting to leave Washington D.C., I noticed the pilot talking to the tower, while being navigated by the crew on the ground. I thought to myself, this one plane has to go through so many instructions and directions, just to take off. I was able to comprehend that the ground crew could see and navigate what was happening in the direct area. They were making sure no accidents or mistakes took place within the immediate range of the plane. The crew in the tower were the ones who saw in the distance, which planes were landing and which planes were taking off. They could see planes on the radar that were miles and miles from the area. They knew when it was safest for us to enter onto the runway for our departure. There were eyes everywhere; they could even tell when we were approaching a storm and what altitude to fly to avoid the storm. This communication was necessary so that the pilot wouldn't be flying blindly at any point. Well, when it comes to purpose and it taking flight, we must have that same continuous communication, so that we won't be moving blindly. The great thing for us is that we have someone in the tower that not only sees the beginning of the flight, but also sees the end before we ever leave the ground. He can instruct us, so that we execute our departure and arrival with precision. Doesn't it make sense to check with our "Tower God" before, during, and after our flight?

Life Behind The Wall

After running through life falling and failing, how do we overcome the mental wall that we have built? The wall which locks us away from purpose, keeping us safely secured in a complacent state. This wall now stops us from trying because we have developed a fear of reaching beyond this wall, because we refuse to fail ever again. Sadly, this wall imprisons us with the reality of what we know we should be doing, imprisoning our purpose and our dreams. We adjust to do other things, while complacently working within this wall, yet our freedom lies beyond. We can see other people outside of the wall walking in the freedom of their purpose. We see the enjoyment of their fulfilled days, as they live beyond the barriers of any self inflicted imprisonment. Day after day, we awake living within the created perimeters and limitations that we have imprisoned ourselves with. Therefore, the question is no longer "Is there a wall, but rather are we planning on dying behind this wall?" Sadly we die, never having taking the opportunity to smell the flowers of purpose or having traveled the highway of fulfillment. Above all, do we plan to continue to live in this world where no one knows we exist? Have we become so institutionalized that even when opportunity presents itself, we chose the familiar restrictions of the wall over the freedom of what purpose can bring? Our lives behind the wall have served the purpose of dictating our past, our present, and possibly our future, yet never the true purpose. Unfortunately, we cease to grow because we cease to venture. We have learned to live comfortably within the high walls of past failures and present uncertainties. As a result, we walk these perimeters often associating ourselves with only those who speak our language and support our imprisonment. At the sight of anyone who speaks of freedom and their plans to obtain it, we withdraw simply because it reminds us of the possibilities beyond the wall. I have found that the wall will always be there as justification. However, we must come to realize that it is our birthright to live a life of freedom, exploration and discovery. Therefore, if this is something that we think about, then it must be possible, and if it is possible, then we should let faith lift us up over the wall that we would embrace and live in the freedom of purpose.

CHAPTER 3

IT BELONGS TO YOU.

PURPOSE IS A PERSONAL THING

What's Your Drink?

W e all have a drink that we thirst for, be it's something cold, wet, and refreshing or something hot, smooth, and creamy. Whatever our drink is; Kool-Aid, hot chocolate, pop, or the cool fresh taste of water, when we drink this liquid fulfillment, it quenches every nerve of thirst. No matter what time of the day, this drink hits the spot, it's right on time. In the same manner as our physical thirst, we have an internal thirst that needs quenching. It longs for that one thing that can cool the internal flame of unfulfillment. The internal thirst seeks that which has the ability to quench the dry hot void of unfulfillment, as it empowers, soothes, and pushes us to the highest degree of motivation. This soothing drink of choice can be warmly sipped on a cold and rainy day, as it fulfills us internally with the assurance of tomorrow. We can embrace it at the end of the day as night falls, as it helps us to be at ease; enforcing rest as a result of our day being fulfilled. This drink can also be shared in company, as we watch the eyes of those around us light up. It can also be the warm cup of reality that stems a conversation within ourselves as we sit alone. This drink that I'm speaking of is purpose, that wonderful thing which was designed and prepared just for you. While others may tend to have a taste for it, when you drink it, it fulfills your deepest personal thirst. As a matter of fact, just like that liquid drink of choice, purpose becomes something that we look forward to. It's sometimes the only thing that tends to help quiet the noise of internal and external commotion. It becomes a sip of empowerment as we greet morning and the sweet taste of fulfillment as the curtains of night fall. It is filled with nutrients that nurture and empower the internal body, as it adds years of life and energy, causing us to live to the fullest. Best of all, it is enriched with vitamins H and S (Happiness and Satisfaction), as it takes the tired and weary and rejuvenates them back to life. Purpose is a worldwide drink; individually tailored and prepared. Purpose is the aroma that awakes many and the daily fulfillment that allows us to rest. However you prepare and serve it, purpose is something that motivates our morning, directs our day and closes our night. What a powerful and refreshing drink to a wandering and thirsty soul. Will you let the cool, sweet nectar of purpose cool your dry thirst of unfulfillment? To all my purpose fulfilled brothers and sisters I raise the glass of purpose and say, CHEERS!

Are People Suppose To Understand?

Be committed and immovable in fulfilling your purpose. If you are expecting a great support system along your journey to purpose, you may need to prepare yourself to sometimes stand-alone. When it comes to purpose and it's great reality, there may be very few who will be able to really identify with its actual existence, especially if we are trying to fulfill that which is uncommon to the group of immediate people who we are accustomed to associating with. Humorously speaking, how can we speak of going to the moon while surrounded by those who are earth bound? Seriously, when you think about it, how long did it take some of us to realize the gift and purpose that existed right within us? So, it should be of no surprise that others might fail to see it. In fact, even when we try to describe the vivid reality of that which has now been exposed to our inward sight or repeat what we hear internally, it often won't make total sense. This can be the reality that we face also with our loved ones as they try to understand, but sometimes find it difficult. For many, seeing the internal fire that we feel and know to exist can be but a strongly voiced reality. If we are fortunate, some of us may be blessed with special people in our lives, be it family or friends who because of their own encounters of such, may sense the familiar flow of brewing purpose ready to erupt. What I have found is that people may tend to hold to certain characteristics that we presented prior to the embracing of our purpose. If we have lived a life of complaining, doubt, and fear it is often hard for others to shake that image of us, even after now having discovered our purposed filled potential. Furthermore, if those around us have known or watched us long enough to see our falls and failures, this becomes what we're measured by. In Matthew chapter 13 verse 57, Jesus said, "A prophet is not without honor, except in his own country and his own house." This means that we may find greater support from those who don't know our past or shortcomings. Fortunately, they only see our present state of blessedness, as purpose shows forth through us. While those who have watched our past external inability may continue to find it hard to see and embrace our true internal purposed ability. There are times when we will find that the only true supporter of the unseen lies in the unseen, which is the spirit man. This spirit that God placed in each of us speaks of greater things. These are things which it divinely sees, that which we are destined to do. Some call this internal acknowledgment a hunch, a funny feeling, or a crazy thought. As a result, it is ignored or maybe periodically pondered upon, but never seriously embraced for its complete empowerment. The reason this reality seems unreal is that it's not visible nor does it often equate to where we are in life or where we have been. Therefore, in saving ourselves of any added doubt and hindrance, we must be very careful in whom we share this treasure with, if we must! Above all, I believe that we should let the manifestation of this blossoming power, bloom into a reality that will brighten even the darkest doubtful mind. And then, maybe the reality of who we were versus who we have become through purpose, will help those around us understand and believe in the greater power of purpose that exist in all of us.

Be True to Your Gift

There are a lot of people in this world who are intoxicated with the life of someone else. Often this drunkenness is based on public image, fame, and fortune. These people are mesmerized to the point that they literally ignore that which they were giftedly designed to do. Many of them have set out on a spellbinding mission to become someone else regardless of what it takes. Now don't get me wrong, it's great to use the energy of others that we may see to help motivate and inspire us to obtain our purpose. Unfortunately, the problem is that many seekers, especially our children, are smothering their divine gifts in an attempt of drunken hope and wishfulness to become someone else.

While there are a few who share the same level of talent as some of the celebrities and may reach stardom, the harsh reality is that everyone will not play in the NBA. Many will not have a number one hit on the radio, or star in an international movie, no matter how many lessons are taken or how much we practice. God made all of us unique, blessing each of us with a special gift. He made us talented in a way that may bring light to one or thousands. Our objective must be to find out what it is that we possess and learn how to embrace and nurture it. Above all, we must be determined to remain true to it, for in it is the fulfillment for our life and possible the energy for someone else's. Amazingly, there are those who mimic the lives of others and do break onto the stage of stardom. However, the story too often ends the same, as many of these people sadly find out that what they thought they wanted was but an illusion of someone else's happiness. They find themselves stressed, miserable, and unfulfilled, lacking the drive and fulfillment to maintain. These people realize that they chased the flicker of an image, instead of the fire of a purpose.

I believe purpose is a seed covered and protected by God, as it is carefully placed within each of us. However, only the few who truly seek to know and embrace it are the ones that gain total access and empowerment of it. It is not something that you can partially embrace, for this gift gives life in accordance to the life it's given. Simply spoken, if you are true to it, it will be true to you.

In 1st Corinthians chapter 10 verse 23, this scripture can help you to understand and focus. It reads, "all things are lawful for me, but all things are not expedient: all things are lawful for me, but all things edify not." Translation; we can do anything that we want to do, but not everything that we do is helpful in creating the essence of who we are to be; we can do anything we want to do, but not everything that we do helps in unlocking, nurturing and releasing the power of the true person that we are designed to be. We must not swing as to fight, but we must strike to win. Chose this day "your" weapon and make "your" aim clear and accurate.

The Light of Truth

I have come to realize that the greatest crime a person can ever commit against himself or herself, is trying to be someone else. When you think about it, we heard this all the time coming up as kids from our parents. They often asked us why were we trying to be someone else. The truth of the matter is that other people lives tend to look better or seem easier than ours. Therefore, we never take time to find out who we are or what special gift we have to offer. It's almost like a quiet kid who spends most of his time reading, due to his extreme love for books, a person who we define as a bookworm. Unfortunately, because of these characteristics he is unaccepted and unpopular. As a result of trying to be accepted, he make a drastic decision to join a gang of tough knuckleheads. Once he's in the gang, he seems to act out a sense of toughness and daringness. His new found image and power surge pushes him to the front of the stage. However, my question becomes, "is this new sense of power because of his internal makeup or is it due to the illusive presence of what seems to be the greater force?" Do you think once he goes home at night, that he's there thinking about the schemes the gang and him are going to pull off on the next day? Or could he possibly be in his room consumed by the opportunity to read one of his favorite books? The external power exists only when he is surrounded by the supporting element, but once he's alone, he is who he is! The true power is the power that exists regardless of external surroundings.

I came to an amazing discovery while working in a prison outreach program back in 1999. When visiting some of the inmates, I was surprise to find that a lot of them had return to what I call their pure age ambitions. This is the time of our life when we only see what we feel. It is the time in which we talk about what we hear from within, glassy eyed children who dream of being astronauts and firemen. It's the moments in our life where the truth within us is so powerful that it makes us feel as if we can fly to the moon. Amazingly, here you had people that were arrested for gang violence, robbery, and other crimes, but it wasn't until they were incarcerated that they began to draw, write poetry, or release other internal gifts. You see, when they were on the streets, they drew to the element that seemed the strongest, denying that which could have been within. However, once incarcerated with nothing but time to spend with self, they were once again able to hear the lost voice within. The sad thing is that the truth was within all along, but they chose to grab hold of that which appeared more powerful. As a result, it wasn't until their incarceration that they discovered the true power of their artistic talent, the intensity of their poetic ability and the reality of their true ambitions.

Sometimes the light can be seen and other times it's forced into recognition, either way, we are who we are. It is a great misfortune to find that we have smart people living foolishly, extraordinary people settling for ordinary things, and those empowered with visions and dreams only reaching for that which is within arms reach. I believe that when we are true to that which is within, that which silently makes us who we are, then we will draw unseen powers to be. Whether these powers come in the form of opportunities, others of the same spirit, or even escorts that will lead us to the higher ground. I truly believe this internal truth draws that which it is. Have you had a heartfelt desire to do something, but you felt like this so called idea was crazy or just stupid? But somehow, maybe by accident someone found out and now the secret was out. The funny thing is that as we stood waiting for judgment to be handed down to us, amazingly enough we found out that we weren't alone in our thinking, and that there were a few others like ourselves. It may seem that sometimes we are the only one on the planet with such insane ideas, but when we release our power it will find its way to that which it is. I never knew there were so many writers, until I started talking about the books, which I was writing. The truth of what we are has the power to stand alone, while yet drawing the energy of the same truth. I leave you with this thought, "If you died tomorrow, would your greatest sorrow be from the things you failed at, or would it be from what you knew to be true, but refused to attempt."

Purpose and Grace

Let's fantasize for a moment. You just won a hundred thousand dollar sports car in a contest. Due to all the special features for this car, it won't be finished for another 90 days. Let's also say that in 90 days, the only thing you have to do is go to the dealership, show your I.D., and the car is yours. Guess what, because this is a fantasy the 90 days are up; so it's off to the dealership! You walk into the showroom drooling, you show your I.D., they give you the keys, escort you to the car, and wave bye-bye. At this point life couldn't get any better. Now, you are sitting in this hundred thousand dollar rocket launcher with a Grinch that stole Christmas grin on your face, suddenly it dawns on you that you don't know anything about this car. The contest said you won the car, but it never said anything about instructions or a class pertaining to the car, hopefully they threw in an owner's manual. So, Mr. or Mrs. Prize Happy based on the scenario I just described, you now have possession of a "Stealth Bomber," but don't know how to use it. Without proper instructions and understanding, you probably won't even be able to start this car, due to the special design of the hidden ignition. What about the anti-theft device, the navigation system, or the possible list of cautions pertaining to the car? If you are not careful you could hurt yourself or worse. I can imagine by now that everyone at the dealership is grinning, as you sit there; frustrated, feeling stupid, unable to even start the car. What I'm trying to get you to understand is that even with this great gift, without understanding or help from the manufacturer, this beautiful blessing is "useless". In fact, if by chance you got this car started and got it off the lot, you would never maximize its total performance ability without instructions.

Well, in the same manner, purpose without God's grace can be even more frustrating without intricate instructions. Grace is where God intercedes and leads. Most importantly, this is the way we gain understanding of the special gift in which God has given each of us. We can gain understanding of its purpose and how to nurture and maximize it to its fullest potential. It is God's grace that helps to shine light on the direction in which we must go with our purpose. Therefore, when it comes to purpose; like having ownership of the car, it is a must that we get with the manufacturer to gain total understanding of our gift and how to properly use it. I believe there are a lot of gifted people in this world who see their purpose; however, they don't know how to nurture their gift or what direction to take it. Therefore, they spend years sitting idle on their gift, possessing full potential to take off, but never going anywhere. There is no way around it, only by the Creator's grace can we truly and fully enjoy our gift. Sadly to say, I have seen many gifted people who had great purposes struggled to the point of exhaustion trying to reach their destination. But fortunately, once they sought God the Giver of the gift, they found direction, endurance, and clarity to accurately move forth. To simply put it, our strenuous efforts often lead us along the long route, around the house and through the back door. While, all along God is seeking to show us how to enter gracefully through the front door. We forcefully try to crawl through any opening we can find, while God says follow me through to the dining table. The gift is definitely a blessing, but access and understanding are also vitally important. When I speak of understanding, I am simply paralleling this to the layout. This is where we find full clarity in our total purpose; such as I know I can write music, but should I be singing also? I know I have a love for cooking, however, am I to own a restaurant? A lot of times we short change our-selves, because we fail to get an intimate layout of our total purpose. We take the milk but leave the cow! Are we maximizing our gift to the fullest or are we settling for the minimum?

The book of Proverbs tells us that "knowledge is great, but in all thy getting get understanding." It's great to have knowledge of your gift, but it's even better to have understanding in how to skillfully use it. Purpose and grace is the combination that makes a success sandwich taste great.

The Rain

I'm reminded of a story that I know will be a blessing of empowerment to you, pertaining to the coming of the rain. The story is Noah's Ark. God told Noah to build an ark of great proportion, and based on translation, the ark was believed to be 450 ft. long, 75 ft. wide and 45 ft. high. God told Noah to build this ark because he was going to send rain that would flood the earth. Now there are several points in this biblical story that ran though my mind. First, an ark of this size was going to take some time, therefore in all the days that Noah worked, the earth would have to stay dry. Secondly, an ark this size was definitely noticeable to the public, so what would they think? Would he tell them of God's plan and if so, would they think he was crazy? And thirdly, which is also often our struggle, in regards to Noah being called for something so great, but possibly questioning it. You see, when you look at the setting of this whole situation, Noah was put on the spot. He would have to go against what people thought of him, including friends and relatives pertaining to such a ridiculous idea. Noah would also have to work very hard with a task of this size, while all along never seeing a drop of rain to confirm his task. Noah would have to fight every inner demon, every fear, and every obstacle to accomplish the internal purpose that he knew to be true. Can you imagine what this guy had to face?

I believe that the power of purpose is identified when we face others and ourselves for the sold-out belief of our destiny. Often times like in this story, we know that we know, that we have been called to do something certain, without a doubt. However, the task becomes overcoming fear, pride, distractions, people, and self. When we look at the size of God's plan for Noah's life and for some of ours, it's one thing to have a personal mission, but it's something else to know the mission will affect the lives of others. Most of all, what about often times having to diligently work without a sign of rain. This can be frustrating, because at times the mission can outright not make sense. Sometimes there is a need for a sign or something to let us know that we are not imagining our purpose or going crazy. It is during these times, we just have to believe in the internal voice of God pertaining to his purpose for our lives. We must stay focused and labor through the often cloudiness of our minds, the heaviness of our hearts, and the fear of the unknown. The greatest factor of this story for me was, "that God didn't send the rain until Noah was finished building the ark". I truly believe with all my heart, this is the most important factor that we must lock in on; that sometimes we want the rain to come, before we have done our part of the plan. To simply put it, if God had sent the rain before Noah was finished, it would have destroyed everything including the ark. God wants us to work our part of purpose, to make sure it is as "air tight" as possible. Therefore, when God sends the rain, the outside forces won't seep through. He wants us to work at a pace that's diligent but not careless, so that our arks are solid in everyway. If you want to be detailed about this story, I believe that even if the sky had become cloudy too soon, Noah may have become panicky and speeded up causing him to carelessly put the ark together. This same thought needs to be considered as a reality in our lives, while we are working during the dry days.

What would happen right now, if while you are studying the blueprint of your purpose, gathering supplies together and diligently working on your ark, that opportunity came too soon? Would you move prematurely? Would you be fully prepared for what you must face? Would the presentation of yourself and purpose be "airtight?" For some reason we think God has different rules for different people, but believe me God has been in the purpose building business for a long time. He knows the time in which to send rain that will carry us and our ark to the prepared destination. I will close this vital lesson by saying this; the purpose for Noah was so great that God couldn't allow any mistakes. He knew the person he was using and all that was needed, including the time. God doesn't make mistakes, so if he has called you to do something, regardless of how large or small, he knows all that is needed and the time to send the rain. The greatest task of purpose is being mature enough to work it, regardless of judgment, embarrassment, or validation. There aren't too many men who could have fulfilled the purpose that God chose for Noah, that's why this was Noah's purpose. Most Importantly, there aren't too many people who can fulfill the purpose that God has chosen for you. You should feel special that God sees something in you, which enabled him to call you for a special mission. Though the days may be dry and hot and there's not a cloud in the sky, if you know that you are working on your purpose, be strong and patient, for the rain will come!

CHAPTER 4

LIVE I SAY!

YOUR PURPOSE WILL GIVE LIFE TO YOU AND THOSE AROUND YOU.

The Contractions Are Getting Stronger

You've embraced your purpose and dream to find out that it's not only real, but that it has also brought life to you. As a result, you now feel something powerful living within you that's changing your attitude, your belief and your perception of self. You didn't know that you could fulfill this internal thing, but now it's happening. In fact, the more you do it, the stronger it gets. You feel the jolt of it pulling as it demands more and more. Even when you try to slow down and give it rest, it refuses to stay within, for it is determined to come out. At first, it all seemed like only a quaint idea, kind of faint, but now it has created life inside you. You are pregnant with it and you can't deny it. Some notice it and some don't! Nevertheless, it doesn't matter because you know! Just like a natural pregnancy, this internal life is starting to change your external features. You don't walk the same, you don't sound the same, there's even a glow about you. To simply explain it, you have now become full! You have become so internally filled with the reality of your gift, your destiny, and your purpose, that it's starting to overflow into your external life. You now find yourself locked away with this life listening, as it instructs, demands, and fights for existence. Even when you try to leave it for just a moment for outside interests, you hear it calling and tapping on your heart. Apparently, contractions become stronger when we are reaching the point of delivery. In other words, when that life within us is becoming full grown, it must be brought forth into the external. As these contractions become stronger, you will find that as doctors assist in delivery, there will be those who will help you with the delivery, be it in the simplest form. The contractions will become even more painful as you realize you can no longer hold purpose inward, that you must now push and give external life to that which has been breeding within. In fact, if you don't push it, it will push you! Contractions are a beautiful thing; for they tell us that not only is there life inside of us, but also that the time is nearing for us to bring forth the internal power, which we possess. Wow! Pain with a purpose!

The Blessing Of Purpose

As I observe people in this day and time, it seems there is an intense hope that we have for something to happen in our lives. It is as if we are waiting for a miracle of some sort to take place that will change the way things are. We hope and pray that God would come and relieve us from the burden of our ordinary but pressured lives. We seek with an earnest appetite to be delivered from the mechanical and routine pace in which we're operating. Above all, we stand in hope of being blessed with something that will propel us into the ultimate level of happiness. The amazing thing I have discovered is that we are looking for something that we already possess. Each of us has been blessed with a gift, a purpose for living. We have been blessed with something that will enhance and make a difference in the lives of others. Whether this be in the life of one or the lives of one-thousand, we all possess a gift within us, which is to be a contribution during our stay here on earth. The gifts of God are remarkable being that they not only can cause others to be blessed and prosper, but simultaneously cause prosperity in our lives as well. These gifts can range from cooking, singing, public speaking, poetry, the gift of working with people, and a variety of other arts. We seek to have a miracle take place in our lives, however the miracle often comes through tapping into that which we already possess. As a result, we will begin to watch miraculous changes take place in our lives, as we grab hold to the magic of our gift. I have found that one reason many of us can't find the true fulfilling change we are looking for is we aren't aware or informed of the gift we possess. Therefore, we walk around unhappy and living beneath our potential in every aspect of our lives. We have jobs but are not fulfilled; we make money but often at a miserable cost. Meanwhile, within each of us is the key that will unlock the door to the life in which we were designed to live. As we pray and hope for a response from God, God seeks for a response from us. This is evident in the Bible; in James chapter 2 verse 17, which states, "Faith without works is dead." In other words God has given us a powerful seed that if we cultivate it and work it, it will bring forth fruit. The sad thing is we have a garden, but chose to starve! We have great treasure within us, but remain poor and without. Therefore, unless we dig to expose the gift that God has instilled within us, we will remain unfulfilled, unhappy and unempowered. I believe the only thing that stands between many of us and prosperity is being true to who we are internally. Most Importantly, we must recognize and unlock that which we have been called to be. If God placed the seed within us, then it's there for a reason. That which we are seeking in hope that we would be free, is within us seeking to be freed.

The Memory of You

If you died today, what would you be remembered for? Would you be remembered for the great empire that you left behind? Or maybe you'll be remembered by the great estate sitting on top of the hill, which serves as an icon of who you were. Perhaps there's a secret safe within the wall of your house which holds great family fortune. While these may be the dramatic scenes scripted in some of the great Hollywood flicks, lets deal with the truth pertaining to us. I'm talking about the ones who have yet to make a million, the ones whose houses are on a neighborhood street and not on an isolated hill, or the ones who may leave a great bill instead of a great will. If we knew we were going to die today, the only thing that would be left behind would probably be a letter that held the statement, "If I had another chance to live life over, I would live it different, more intimately." What I am saying is that often we make the decision that as soon as we strike it big, we will create something that will serve as an icon of who we were. Unfortunately, this is often a marker created by money, assets and material images. Sadly to say, while we spend most of our lives waiting for this moment, we miss out on giving the greatest contribution that can be given by us, which is what we were "purposed" to give. I'm speaking of the gift that is part of our birthright while living upon this earth. The gift, which was specially designed for us to touch the lives of those, assigned to our lives. There are people out there whether family, friends, or total strangers, waiting to know our names and to simply be empowered by the gifted energy we possess.

    Though we may not leave millions, there is something that will cause those left behind to smile or deeply sigh at the thought of what we did. Most importantly they will have been blessed by the difference we made in their lives. There is a poem which comes to mind, that occupies the walls of many people's homes called Footprints, and though we have never met the author of this poem, he has impacted our lives greatly by his words. I think of the great internal joy and fulfillment he must possess knowing that he contributed such a life empowering gift to many. However, as with this anonymous author, due to the massive impact that our gifts sometimes have, we may never receive direct gratitude from all those who we have touched. But, we can receive the personal blessing of knowing that we were the ones who bought hope and help in the lives of those around us. It is each person's personal aspiration as to whether they are to be openly gratified or personally fulfilled. We may leave a legacy noticed by all or a simple memory to our loved ones of the fulfilled life we lived in trying to touch others. Nevertheless, whatever we do, let it be done in such a way that our memory is etched into the hearts of those who we leave behind, not so much visually, but more so internally. For an internal memory is forever etched in love, but an external memory erode with time.

Unspoken Identity

Do you know that your gift and purpose can identify you long before your actual name is known? It's that thing that you are identified by long before you are formally introduced. You will find that people will often ask, "Aren't you that guy who writes poetry or "aren't you that young lady who sings?" Believe me this is not an insult, if anything this is a compliment, because often there are by-standers who have never gotten close enough to be personally introduced, but by our gift we are recognized. Perhaps it could be through word of mouth, for when the fire of purpose illuminates you, the word spreads. In addition, some may not have witnessed our talent and bestowed grace, but have experienced the reality of it from the praise of others. Many artists; be it musicians, writers, singers or even athletes, are often never seen directly by their future managers or supporters, but it is through the verbally painted picture of others that serve as a representation of them. What we possess and deliver often speaks louder and greater than we ever could.

Take for instance a classroom full of students, on the first day they all appear evenly matched, however, in due time it is the internal power that illuminates from certain students that tells the teacher whose who. It is the uniqueness, that inner melody that causes what's ordinarily delivered by most, to be extraordinarily delivered by others. Furthermore, if we were to meet and greet a hundred people, few would remember us. But, if our inner possession was singing and we sang a song of the soul, we would be engraved in their hearts forever. We all possess an inner talent, a gift and purpose, which tells those around us to take notice, without us ever having to say a word. This internal possession can take that which is externally lacking and unrecognizable and drape us with a light of empowerment that says, "I'm special and uniquely created." This internal empowerment doesn't necessarily have to be an athletic or musical empowerment, by no means am I saying that. What I am saying, is that whatever it is that you possess; be it a spirit of kindness, encouragement, or love for life and people, let it be the identifying marker that presents you to the world. Some of the greatest people I've ever met were everyday people who possessed a light that commanded attention. These lights have been so powerful that when I describe these people to others, though they had never personally met them, there was an appreciation and acceptance by the transferred presence of who they were. So, now that you know the unspoken speaks loud, "who are you and what is it that you possess?" Be it big or small, what is it that tells others of your uniqueness and beautiful empowerment? Our mouths may say hello, but our presence says, "I'm here!"

The World's Blueprint

From the beginning of time to this present day, man has used his individual ideas in helping to create the blueprint for this world. These were the burning ideas and visions that man saw within himself, that he would contribute to the world. However, if we were to look back at some of the seemingly foolish ideas of times past, we would probably laugh, due to our high-tech and intellectual minds of this time. Fortunately, the foolish idea of one person, pieced together with someone else's foolish idea, is what has made this world what it is today. We live in a vast world of choices; ranging from the food we eat, the music we listen to, the way we communicate, to the clothes we wear. Each of these things were individual contributions shared within the melting pot of our global lives. Today we can take something as simple as a cigarette lighter, and never give a second thought in reference to it's beginning. But, can you imagine the response it probably got when it was first introduced? I mean imagine the thought of creating a hand held device, which contained a chemical mixture and a mechanism that would make fire readily accessible to us whenever we needed it. Can you imagine those who were initially introduce to this idea? They probably wondered at the time, was there such a great need in their lives that they needed to carry around fire. The answer is, "a definite yes," by votes of the cigarette makers and cigarette smokers, and by the camper isolated a hundred miles from the rest of the world. For him this device would help to provide effortless light and heat. In fact, back in the early years of man, the cigarette lighter would have been a great benefit, being that fire was the only source of light and heat. So, while the use for a cigarette lighter may not have made total sense initially, this foolish little idea has proven to be most necessary.

In the same manner as our easy access to fire through the cigarette lighter, we have accessibility to almost anything we need even when it comes down to comfort. We all have an internal need to be soothed physically, spiritually, emotionally and mentally. One of the popular ways we obtain the mental and emotional soothing that we need is through music. Believe me our choices are wide, because of someone's crazy idea that his New Orleans flow would be received and accepted by those who unknowingly had an appetite for something called, the blues. Well, now days we also have selections ranging from gospel to jazz and hip-hop to rock, all a result of individually started ideas. No one was really sure where any of these would go, but there was a thirsty world out there that needed soothing. In fact, hip-hop of all music was initially looked upon as silly and totally absurd. But today, some of it has become the powerfully recognized voice and identity of many of our young people and a few of our old. Furthermore, even when we look around our world today at the many high tech gadgets and accessories available, we often fail to realize that these all started initially as the wild or crazy thoughts of one person, which now play roles in all of our lives.

Our personal mission must become to intensely search ourselves to find that which we possess? What ideas do we have, what contributions lie within us; that we believe will make a difference in someone's life? Our biggest problem is because these ideas often come from us, we believe they are but foolish thoughts. We wonder how our little unknown selves, could ever contribute to the enormous melting pot of the world. Nevertheless, when you think about it, the world's melting pot with its vehicles, communication devices, entertainment, clothing and various other contributions were formed by individuals just like you and I. Although we see the finished product with the lights and the glitter, which is pretty much the public presentation of these contributions, they started off as a single idea by someone like you and I. In addition, it has been people like you and I that have added to the improving of individual ideas and inventions that exist. In this world we all can make a contribution, whether it's to bring into existence that needed something for a few lives or to add a piece to the puzzle of life; we all have something. Can you imagine with all the inventions, foods, literature, and other everyday things that are part of our life; if each person had said, " this sounds foolish, I'll wait or pass on this idea"? We would still be walking around bare foot, eating raw meat, and still on horseback, living a very primitive lifestyle. But fortunately, because of those like you and I, they took an internal vision; an idea and pushed and pushed and pushed, until it became a manifested reality. There is a saying by the great writer Myles Monroe, to paraphrase, who said, " some of the greatest inventions, music and ideas lie in the graves with the men who possessed them". It is my saying, as I speak this hopefully to receiving hearts, "If you feel the fire of a vision, then it must be there with a purpose." One mans' foolishness, is possibly another mans' hope.

The Walk – The Reward

There was a man who wanted to start a seashell collection, so one day he decided to go to the beach with his backpack and gather shells. As the man walked along the beach among the many vacationers, he spotted a nice shell every now and then. However, as he proceeded to walk a little farther, he began noticing more beautiful and unique shells. After he had walked about twenty minutes, he came to a place where there seem to be shells everywhere. The man became very excited and began grabbing the shells and gently tossing them in his backpack. After a while the man looked up and realized he had walked for miles to a place where he was the only one around. When he looked back, he could only see vague images of the distant people along the shore. The man wondered, "How could he have walked so far?" For a minute the man became frustrated, because it had gotten hot and he was already tired. Most of all, the man knew that he had to travel the long distance back. The man decided to sit down for a moment and rest, while he examined his shells. When he removed his backpack and looked inside, to his surprise he had gathered more shells than he realized. He began emptying them on the ground and was amazed at the beauty and color of all the shells he had. There were orange ones, white ones, and blue-striped ones in all shapes and sizes. It was at that moment that he realized, in him being so preoccupied with gathering the shells that he had paid no attention to how far he walked. After sitting and admiring his treasure, he came to realize two things. First, he realized the walk couldn't be compared to what he had gained. Secondly, if he had not wandered as far as he did into this uncharted area then maybe his findings wouldn't be so precious and rewarding.

You see, sometimes in life, our mission will cause us to journey for days, months, and even years. As a result, at some point, we may look up to realize that we have walked or even crawled for quite some distance. This can place us in a position, which at times, we are isolated from others. The wonderful thing however, is that if we will sit down for a moment and look within we will be surprised to find that we have gathered a vast collection of treasure. This collection may consist of wonderful people in our lives, knowledge, wisdom, and even moments of small but empowering accomplishments.

The walk may have been long and we may even be tired, but in comparison to what we have gained there is no comparison. If you are tired and it seems that you have been walking for miles, look within, I believe you will be pleased to see what you have gathered. Often we spend so much time looking at the reality of our weary external journey that we forget to stop and look at the priceless achievements and accomplishments that we now possess. The reward is many times found during the walk.

Breathe!

Discovering my purpose was one of the greatest things that ever happened to me. As a result of this empowering discovery, I realized the importance of not only discovering my purpose, but also the need in helping others to discover and understand their purpose as well. Purpose is an extremely important part of life. We cannot afford to let anything stop us from fulfilling it. We must be balanced in embracing the highs and pressing through the lows, that we would add our part to the blueprint of life. I believe this segment of the book will be one of the most intricate parts in helping you along your journey. You may find yourself returning to this segment again and again.

My biggest contribution to you here, lies partly in a brief story about two friends at a funeral. The story takes place with a young man who was experiencing great grief at his close friend's funeral. His friend was a true comrade and support in his life. While standing alone mourning, he was approached by another friend who sought to comfort him during this trying moment. With great pain in his eyes and agony in his voice, he looked up and asked his friend, "How do I get through this?" His friend replied with great compassion and power "<u>you keep breathing</u>, that's how you get through this". Most importantly he said, "<u>you must take</u>

every breath, forfeiting none of them". That's the story.

Now if you missed this powerful point, let me break it down for you. We must breathe in the mist of adversity and in the mist of pain, and with the committed determination to press on, take every breath that awaits! We are sometimes faced with challenges in which our eyes overload our thought with overpowering things that we aren't prepared to process. We suck in the whole reality of the visual situation without the thought of any possible hope to come. This forces our mind to panic, sending pressure to our heart; which like poisonous gas causes a malfunction in our breathing. Think about it, whenever we mentally face something traumatic our bodies immediately respond to the reality of the situation, often causing a shut down. Now while I am not trying to medically lay out the process, I am trying to make the point that our mind overloads our body, often times congesting us. What we must do however, is regardless to how horrific the situation or sight, claim our breaths and refuse suffocation. I have seen dogs with their heads out the car window and somehow, no matter how fast the car was going or the wind was blowing, they forced a breath in. Sometimes life can bring so much with its seemingly everlasting illusions, that it can cause a suffocating affect. Life's situations have a smothering affect on our breathing, which stops us from moving, which eventually stops us from existing.

This illustration can be taken metaphorically or to a certain degree literally. When a person has a panic attack they have to concentrate in order to regain their normal breathing pattern. In the same manner, we must focus and breathe ourselves right into another minute, another hour and eventually into another day. We cannot let certain temporary delivered realities choke out our existence. We must believe with each breath that circumstances can and are changing.

A funny conversation that I had with some friends comes

to mind about this very thing. One day we were all talking about the childhood memory of waking up in the middle of the night and seeing the illusive sight of a coat hanging on the door or a shirt lying on a chair. Amazingly, as children these objects seem to come alive, as we awaken in the dark late night. In fact, we laid there in anticipation of eventually being overtaken by these night monsters. If some of you can remember back to these moments, you will remember how the sight of these objects literally verbally choked us, freezing us in fear. After our momentary panic attack however, we would force ourselves to take in a breath strong enough to let out a scream of, "helpppp!" Immediately, our mom or dad would come running in and turn on the light to expose, you got it, "the coat monster." Can you imagine, never being able to take that breath, to deliver that cry? We would have lain there in that bed with our heads under the blanket and emotionally died or fell asleep, which ever came first.

Well, this is also paralleled with life itself because sometimes the initial sight of things can make us cover our heads, stop breathing, and refuse to move. But when we take that breath, it allows us to take a step, which allows us to proceed on and exist another day. This is one of the reasons why suicide is so common. People get to a place where situations and circumstances overtake them, mentally and then emotionally. As a result, these situations or circumstances with a powerful choking affect, chokes out all hope. Therefore, hope being like oxygen, when it leaves, we struggle to breathe and if we struggle to breathe too long we eventually suffocate.

If I could conclude on any note pertaining to this realistic matter, it would be that there are too many great things in life that await us, which we must fulfill. Therefore, we must keep our eyes on the prize (purpose) and breathe through every situation, right into our destiny!

The Sacrifice

Say what you may, but there's no way around it; purpose is measured by some type of sacrifice. We must get this etched into our minds that we will have to give something to get something. Here, in the United States, I have seen numerous cases where foreigners have come from near and far to take advantage of the wonderful opportunities that we have here. Many of them saw the opportunity and knew if they could get here, no matter what it took, they would succeed. In fact, if it meant that two or three families had to live in one house and combine finances, they would make the sacrifice regardless of the uncomfortable living arrangements. As a result of this momentary sacrifice, these are now some of the business owners in many of our communities. Sadly to say, many of us who have been living here most of our lives will not make any sacrifice of un-comfortableness for the mission of purpose. The bible says in St. Luke, chapter 12 verse 48 "unto whom much is given, of him shall much be required." According to what we want is often on some scale what we must give. This can be the sacrifice of our time, commitment, sleep, or even giving into periods of seclusion and loneliness, just to name a few. I have found that one of our greatest personal rewards is the unseen sacrifice we make to develop and nurture our purpose. As I have said before, we will often find ourselves as mad scientists locked away with only our purpose and ourselves. However, when it's time, we will emerge to deliver that which we are destined to do.

Sacrifices often hurt, make no mistake about it, it's almost like the time during pregnancy. As a result of having a life inside you, at some point you have to give up certain foods, habits, and acts to take on a healthier lifestyle that is conducive with maintaining proper growth of that which is within you. During those months of pregnancy, I have witnessed women speak of the aches and swelling all over their bodies. I have heard them speak of how they had to give up a lot of pleasures, that the baby would be healthy. Well, when it comes to your baby, purpose that is, you will have to sacrifice that it would be healthy and strong. Just like a child that is nurtured properly in the womb, he grows up to be an amazement even to our eyes. In that same manner, when we sacrifice and nurture that which we are called to do, it will grow to amaze us and those around us. Sacrifice is the fee that we pay to apprehend our destiny.

I remember this funny fictional story about a Hawaiian king by the name of King Kahana-Huna. Every year King Kahana-Huna sacrificed a person to the volcano, that the volcano would not erupt and kill everyone in the village. This myth was passed down from his ancestors for hundreds of years. So every year King Kahana-Huna faithfully sought to find the best person to be represented as the sacrifice for the volcano. On the day of the ceremony King Kahana-Huna approached the man whom he chose to be the sacrifice, and asked if he had any last words. The man nervously said yes, and asked the king what did he think would happen if he didn't make the sacrifice. The king simply replied, " that is a great question, unfortunately it is one that won't be answered today." Even in this humorous story there is value, being that in order to gain much you must sacrifice much!

Starving to Live

The man was the sacrificed that the people would live. Most importantly, we must sacrifice now, that many will be blessed later. Sacrifice means sometimes having to die of a few things in our life, that we would live to apprehend the great thing called life. Can you lose to gain?

CHAPTER 5

HOW HUNGRY ARE YOU?

ARE YOU HUNGRY ENOUGH TO DO SOMETHING ABOUT YOUR UNFULFILLMENT?

The Craving

There is a living purpose within many of us that screams with desire for fulfillment. This internal craving can't and won't be silenced, nor will it be fulfilled by anything other than what it internally burns for. As purpose screams within us waiting to be nurtured into life, unfortunately, we continue to starve it, due to the fear and uncertainty of whether or not we can obtain that which it needs for fulfillment. We also struggle with the reality of its seemingly unrealistic appetite, due to the fact that the "craving" desires that which is beyond the comfort of our normal reach. As a result, it seems much easier for us to attempt to ignore or override it, rather than to actually surrender to its demands. For example: the aroma to start your own business may consume you, you have unique and intense ideals that will scream to the world your passion for this venture. However, because of fear, uncertainty, or excuses you accept the reachable alternative of working a job similar to that which you were destined to own. Now this is fine if you are trying to learn more pertaining to your particular craving, but never let this be a substitute. You may not realize it, but we can become unconsciously trapped and begin to justify by saying things like, "well, this may not be exactly what I want but it's close enough." Dreams and purpose were never given to be lived out partially or almost. The thing that makes them the precious internal empowerment that they are, is the fact that they were tailored and uniquely designed just for you. There is no substitute! In fact, you will even find that in most cases, the substitution for that which you want to do will only remind you more of just how much you desire to do this thing in the unique way that you were called to do it. For within you is the unique reality of how it should look, how it should sound, and how it should be presented to the world. You probably spend more time living in the internal reality of that which you possess than you do externally, because you see the shape, the height and the depth of the glory of that which is within. It's yours and you deserve to fulfill it according to the craving that internally haunts you. Have you ever notice when working in something similar or identical to that which you have been purposed to do, you find yourself internally screaming to make suggestions, but you keep quiet because of the fear of sounding crazy? Or maybe, you know your ideas won't be credited to the fullest as being your ideas. Therefore, you sit holding your breath under someone else's air of accomplishment: miserable or illusively satisfied. We must fulfill the craving that's within us for many reasons. First, because the craving can make our external daily lives very frustrating due to its whining internal pleas for fulfillment. Though we may try to ignore them, we will only find ourselves sitting among others, and as they are describing their desires and dreams, we will painfully be reminded of our own. As a matter of fact, we may even find ourselves sometimes failing to listen to others as they speak because of the loudness of that which is internally within us. We will continuously be reminded as the internal craving screams and taunts us of our mere mediocre lives. It will remind us that we are living below full potential, far from that of enriched purpose and totally outside of our designed destiny. Each of us at some point must come to realize that it takes more energy to deal with this nagging reality day to day, than it probably would take to accomplish our destined desire.

Above all, we must ask ourselves the question. Will we one day find ourselves in our ripe old age sitting on the porch or staring out the window, teary eyed and congested because we realize that we failed to even attempt to fulfill our purpose? Will we look around our homes and bitterly realize that there isn't a solid shred of evidence to show that we even attempted to fulfill the craving? In the event that there is a reminder, it will be the personal marker only to ourselves of that which we desired. Unfortunately at the point of being too late, we will suffer even more because we knew, but we didn't do. The craving won't go away and though we may find substitutions for momentary suppression, it will come back even stronger and louder. Begin this day to search for the total fulfillment of "your craving".

Don't Keep Hitting The Snooze

RRRRRinggggggggg!!!!!!!! Gooood Morning! This is your internal alarm clock loudly reminding you that it's time to get up and go to work on purpose! I advise you not to hit the snooze, for it's time to move NOW! No you can't sleep another hour, another minute, or another second! For the world is waiting for what you owe it!

Have you ever notice that after an actual alarm clock initially goes off and you hit the snooze, the more you hit the snooze button, the weaker it's effect is on our hearing? Eventually we gain an automatic response to cutting it off and become numb to it's sound. We all have an internal alarm, which goes off in our lives, telling us it's time to get up, because purpose needs to be fulfilled. However, we continuously hit the snooze, justifying that we have time or no desire to really get up and fulfill purpose. If we are not careful we can weaken and even quiet this internal power of truth. Many are walking around right this very moment numb to the internal alarm of purpose, which once rang in a fierce attempt to acknowledge its existence. This is so easily done, because we learn to rest in our contentment and lounge in the comfort of merely doing what's necessary for basic living. Therefore, while we sleep through purpose, as its alarm of reality continuously rings; we miss our appointed time of arrival. Eventually, when we finally do awake, it's often times too late.

Purpose is often set to the schedule of our maturity, our development, and even our positioning. The fact of the matter is that many times we are not mature enough to understand what we've been called to do in life. Therefore, there is a time in which we are allotted to mature, that we would be able to see past the external illusion to grasp this internal reality. We must develop in our ability the art of not pushing with mental power or physical might, but rather be led by the divine guidance of that which is within. Finally, there is the great importance of our positioning. There are times in our life where we are too busy chasing the dreams of the majority and searching for the keys of entrance into the club house of the trendsetters. We continuously strain to live our life upon the prepaved path, while dying to our own destination. Unfortunately, it's not until we have exhausted ourselves, tired and weary of the mental and physical chase, that we seclude ourselves to a place of momentary peace. This is often the place and the time in which we find our awaited reality. The reality being that we realize the dreams of others are not fulfilling for us and what they deem as happiness is the energy that often makes only them smile. We also come to realize that the destination, in which others have arrived at, is often thousands of miles away from anything that we can call home. The beautiful thing about purpose is it can be the simplest thing in the eyesight of others, while bringing us total fulfillment and extraordinary happiness.

As long as we lay in the ready made bed of the norm, snuggled in the blanket of a patterned life, continuously hitting the snooze, we will never wake up to experience the call of destiny. Each day that the alarm of purpose goes off internally and we ignore it, is another day that we have lost. Sadly, we wake up one morning and realize that we have overslept in our right to live a fulfilled life of internal happiness and soulful fulfillment. Can we afford to keep hitting the snooze on purpose, just for a few more minutes of accepted comfort? The alarm has sounded, are you listening?

The Program

"Up in the mornin' before day, I don't like it no way! Eat my breakfast too soon, starvin' like Marvin by noon! Cause we're hard-core, Army-all the way!" Fort Bliss, Texas, man I remember the program. When I first arrived there for basic training back in 1983, I thought those Drill Sergeants were mad, out right crazy! I mean what was the point of getting up 3:30 in the morning, stretching, jumping around and then running for miles like we were on some kind of mission or something. Picture in your mind 20 or 30 platoons (groups) of men and women, each platoon possibly consisting of 50 or more soldiers, running around in the paved mountains of Ft. Bliss, Texas. It was one thing to see the reflectors from the soldiers uniforms everywhere as we ran that early in the morning, but then you could hear them yelling or as we called it "sounding off" at the top of their lungs. Let me tell you something, when you have 20 or 30 platoons, with 50 or more soldier in each platoon, all trying to out shout the other platoon, you literally feel the ground under your feet shaking. The first time I saw this, still an undisciplined street guy, I thought this was foolish. Everything in me thought this was foolish; I mean why did I need to get up that early in the morning just to exercise? Wouldn't it be better to let us get a little more sleep, eat breakfast, maybe talk with our buddies for a while as our food digested, and then do a lap or two? Yeah Right! What I didn't know was getting up that early in the rawness of the morning and forcing our bodies to become one with the pure flow of energy that existed at that time of the morning was a powerful thing. This program would dictate how we thought and felt all day long. Don't get me wrong, the first few weeks my body was like, "let's go home!" But after a while, I noticed something started to happen. As I looked around at the guys who had arrived with me on day one, who once stood sluggishly and limp, eyes filled with uncertainty, I now began to see a change. This change was not just in them, but in me also. I could feel something was starting to brew within me. There was a sense of raw power that was now replacing the confusion that once filled our eyes; we were starting to focus. By the 6th or 7th week, I remember a lot of us fighting for the chance to lead our platoon in our early morning runs. In fact, I remember it seemed that the worse the weather elements were, the more powerful our energy was. We even had a song called, "In the early morning rain," where we would literally try to shout the clouds into submission. The program had succeeded. By the time I graduated and went home for two weeks, before my next duty station, I was walking raw energy. I could no longer lie around in bed until mid morning. There was now something about the early morning that intrigued me. The energy of the early morning's flow was pure. I remember literally trying to suck all the energy out of the air before everyone else woke up and starting moving about.

Now with this picture painted, you might think I'm trying to get you to go join the military, but I'm not. What I am saying is, you need to get a program and capture the undisturbed early morning energy. I am talking about, if you want to have channeled energy and understanding that will empower your purpose, then get with the program. This

Starving to Live

means that you may have to go to bed earlier than you've been going most of your life. This may result in the punishment of not being able to watch those after nine (9 pm) shows. Make your mission to get some rest; wake up as early as possible, maybe even do some sit-ups, pushups, or stretch. Then, begin to inhale both physically and spiritually and suck as much of the energy out of the air as possible. Believe me, I am not just saying this; you will be surprised at the power of this undisturbed time of the day. Therefore, as you begin to concentrate on purpose, you will see a world of insight open up to you. By the time everyone else wakes up, you will be standing there with a look on your face as if you have just return from running in the mountains. It's important that we realize that there's power in us and this same power exists around us. Although, as the world becomes busy each day, we become distracted as these distractions congest us internally and externally, jamming the flow between our internal and external power. The key is that we are to bathe in the external energy to helps us unlock our internal energy. Therefore, we must commit ourselves to a program of capturing the external energy, that it would free us internally. I know as you stand here day one, you're just like I was. You're probably saying, "Is he mad, why do I need to get up before the break of day?" The only thing I can say is, "try it." Get you a good night sleep, set the clock for lets say 4:00am or 4:30am. And then, make you out a program which can include coffee, and focus! You will know how long you need to bathe in this morning energy and when you finish, you can do what you may. As a matter of fact you can even go back to sleep after you've accomplished your morning run (mission). If you can! I have come to realize soldiers, that without sacrifice, there is no reward. Welcome to the program!

CHAPTER 6

EXCUSES, EXCUSES.

NO MORE EXCUSE.
GET WHAT'S YOURS

Sleep Won't Do It.

When we reach that point of true internal reality, connecting with purpose, we will find that our spirit becomes very demanding in its cries for fulfillment. In fact, any one intentionally living outside of the destined purpose of this internal empowerment, will find that the internal activity can often times become so bothersome that it actually make us externally weary. For example, imagine trying to solve a complicated geometry problem; you sit at your desk for hours arranging and rearranging different solutions, in an attempt to solve the problem, just to end up still lost to the true solution. After a while you will find that your mind becomes strained and stressed, signaling the body for needed rest. Although many have rested for hours, they have awakened still to face the fact of not being able to solve the problem. Can you imagine having to solve ten of these types of problems, one after another? By the end of the night you would be ten times exhausted and frustrated. This analogy is only a fraction of what purpose can do to the mind and body when we have yet to develop a solution in fulfilling it. We know purpose is there deep within us, but how do we get it out? We hear its cry and periodically envision its vivid reality, but where do we begin? In what direction do we go? Or do we even have what it takes! These taunting questions can bring us to a point where our mind refuses to deal with these mechanics any longer, as our bodies show the need for rest. If for but a moment our body demands that we close our eyes and forget our unfulfillment. Now, let me take a moment to express a most important point about this matter, by no means see this as depression. This is more so a state of internal reality and activity resulting in external fatigue. This is due to the reality that something greater has been called of us and it won't go away, that's evident! No matter how many naps we take, when we awaken, though we may feel refreshed and even relieved, purpose stands waiting. You see, sleep quiets the mind but never the soul. It relaxes the body but never the spirit. For that which is true within us, demands to be heard. I often compare the reality of unfulfilled purpose to having a lion cub as a pet. In the beginning the lion cub is cute and it doesn't seem like it will be that much trouble. However, eventually that cute little cub grows into a gigantic beast of beauty, demanding to be free! In the same manner, purpose in the beginning seems like a cute idea, but when it is full grown within the internal home of our bodies it will no longer be contained. It must be unleashed! If we don't free it, it will roar and rip our peace to shreds. Awaken now and set purpose free!

What Are We Waiting For?

It is amazing; the number of us who believe in God and the divine purpose that he has for our lives. However, most of us don't have the faith to execute that which we know we are to do. If you ask many of us about our purpose, we will tell you in so many words, " I know God has called me to do something great and wonderful, but I am waiting for him to pave the path before I take the journey." We treat our destiny like being called for a job by a client, by asking for front money as a guarantee of security before we start the job. In the same sense, when it comes to our purpose we want God in some kind of way to assure us of our outcome. In many cases we want maximum assurance from God; we want him to build the boat, put it in the water, stir up the wind, and navigate us step by step all the way to our destination. Blessed enough, three of these already exist in our favor; for one the boat (purpose) has already been built. It's that nagging, burning feeling within us that's trying to push us beyond the shallow, into deeper and more meaningful areas of life. Second, it's God's desire to guide us all the way, if we seek and entrust back to him that which he has given us. And finally, we must realize that the wind is already stirring. Although we may not feel it where we are, if we will just believe and put our boats in the water, we will be surprised of the existing force. The wind represents God's power, and it's awesome ability to take our gift to its predestined destination. But sadly to say, "we won't put the boat in the water!" We sit around saying, " I believe, I believe, I believe, the question becomes how much? We believe in the purpose giver, which is God, we even believe in the existence of that which we have been called to do. But do we believe enough "to do something?"

In the book of James (Bible) chapter 2 verse 18, it says, " You say you have faith, but have no works, I will show you my faith by or through my works." The evidence of what we believe is not in what we say, but in what we have done or are doing to expose our faith. Many of us are waiting on God to show us a sign, a flash of light, something signifying us to start our mission. The signal is the hunger, the thirst, the drive, the vision and the power of that greater something that we know and feel. It's that unresting cry within us that's begging for fulfillment, that's the signal! So my question again is, what are we waiting for?

If I can tell you anything personally pertaining to purpose, it would be the intense memory of coming through my recovery period of about 9 months from an almost deadly virus. I had no job, no money, and my family and I were barely getting by. Now if anybody ever had a reason to wait and see what God wanted him to do next, it was me. I remember at times feeling as if I was buried beneath a pile of rubble, wondering how to get from beneath and through all that had happened. One thing that kept agitating me was my half written first book, "A Hunger To Behold." Through all that had happened, with me almost dying, I still had a hunger to write. I could have said, "well God, after all I've been through, I think I'm going to wait for you to show me a sign or something telling me what to do next." Fortunately I didn't, because I realized that even though my life and everything in it had been challenged, I knew internally what

Starving to Live

I was to do. I believed in God and my purpose as a writer. Though I had no external supporting factors that everything was going to be all right, I believe that my intense hunger and thirst to write remained in me for a reason. If God gave this gift to me, then he would see it and me through to our destination. To put it plainly, we all have reasons, fears, or justifications, to say we would rather wait for God and certain assurances before we make our move. I feel the thing that propels God into movement is when we recognize what he has given us, and take it, nurture it and watch him give it light and power. A young man once said, "as long as I stand still I am dead weight to the wind, but if I run fast enough, maybe the wind will catch me and I'll take flight." That young man is me. Our beliefs are often overshadowed by doubt and fear. However, when we act, becoming operative, that's when we become bigger than them. By now many of us should be rounding the corners in the marathon of purpose. If you are not, then you need to ask yourself the question, what are you waiting for?

CHAPTER 7

WHO CARES!

IT DOESN'T MATTER WHAT PEOPLE THINK, WHAT'S BEEN DONE, OR WHAT OTHERS ARE DOING. YOU'VE BEEN CALLED TO FULFILL "YOUR" PURPOSE AND THAT'S ALL THAT MATTERS.

Talk Less and Do More

One of the greatest mistakes that I have found that purpose filled people make is talking too much about the internal fire of our purpose and plans. We often want to share this intimate reality with everybody, in hope that we are not insane, but rather justified sane by others. However, what often happens is this backfires in our face. Being that, unless our vision and purpose is within the scope of what appears to be sound or judgmentally obtainable to those around us, we may gain negativity instead of support.

Take for an instance, we sing on the local level; church, community events, or just for those who are near and dear to us. While within us, we see the vision of where our gift is suppose to be on a national or perhaps global level. How do we convince those who have accepted us as the neighborhood star or hometown's best, that we are now giving our gifted purpose wings and sending it on a boundless mission? As spoken previously, that which God has made is supernatural, and often times cannot be comprehended in the natural according to what is seen. Fortunately though, there are a few like ourselves who have been starving to live and have launched out into the deep, crossing over to the other side. These few do have the ability to recognize in us, that which burns within them; that fire, that passion, and that hunger.

Eventually we must ask ourselves the question, why is it that we insist on talking to people who have proven to have no desire in grabbing the flame of purpose or accepting its reality? We repeatedly seem to want to find validation by those who evidently refuse to fulfill anything greater than what they are comfortably able to reach. Our greatest allies during the intimate and explosive hours of the call to purpose is uniting with people or anything empowering to our belief and purpose. This may be person, place, or thing, that we would find the empowering energy to push us forward. We should begin to find the closest support system where we are, and from there gather allies. If this is limited and few, then we may have to develop the mad scientist mentality; locking ourselves away with that creative purpose and begin to give it life. As a result, amazingly one day we may scream, It Lives, It Lives, Behold It Lives! Most Importantly, whenever we feel the need to talk with anyone to justify ourselves of our purpose and our mission, let this be the time that we do something self supportive. Whether this is to write notes, sketch pictures, or whatever we need to sharpen our skill. That which is within is very empowering when we let it out and allow it to stand face to face with us. This is a way of further nurturing our gift and in turn it will further nurture us. Until we find a circle of purpose filled doers and achievers, often what we now do alone in secret, is the only reality of what we shall later do in the open. Sssshhhhhh! And just do it!

The Cocoon Is Ugly But The Butterfly Is Beautiful!

Here I hang cocooned in uncertainty, squirming in doubt, and unattractive in ability. As a result of being cocooned for so long, when I first come out I may have to crawl initially to get to my destination. But, if you keep your eyes on me long enough you'll see my wings sprout and then I'll take flight as a butterfly. Unfortunately, it's hard for us to face the fact that we must hang in a state of development until we reach maturity. To the lookers, they may only see a ball of bundled uncertainty as the days, weeks, and months pass. They wonder if anything will ever happen for us or if we will ever break free from our cocoon state. Unfortunately, those who watch and judge us only see what's on the outside, while within us there is something taking place. The cocoon is that unattractive outer layer which is visible to the world. It's that noticeable thing which tends to define us for the moment. The hanging represents where we are now, all that is seen in this present time. It is important that we remain in our cocoon stage of development, often sore to the eyes of the judgmental. Internally though, we are getting stronger as we continue to feel the changes taking place. At the first break of opportunity we began to take our new, yet wobbly steps, as we breathe the air of our new surroundings. In fact, even to ourselves we may be a little unsure of our ability, while development is still taking place. Soon we begin to feel the internal power of purpose starting to lift us off our feet, above the negativity, the doubt, and opinions. For purpose has now become the wings of power that are now elevating us to a level of unbelievable assurance and ability. Many now watch in amazement, as to say, "isn't that the same caterpillar that was cocooned but a short time ago? Where did this gifted beauty of potential come from?"

The fact of the matter is, while we aren't sure sometimes why we must hang so long in our unattractive state, I truly believe God is more concerned with what's happening on the inside. Therefore, what appears to be external misery can actually be internal empowerment. The cocoon that houses the butterfly has a set time in which the butterfly and all of its beauty is released into the world. We are released through the beautiful birth of purpose. As a result of this timing, it keeps us from being released malnourished, but rather strong enough to walk and then eventually to fly. So, while the sun pierces through and we seem trapped in a stalemate position, let us be assured that the Creator of cocoons and butterflies has set a perfect time clock in which the beauty of the butterfly will be seen. Not too soon, nor too late.

The Link

In today's society there seems to be a growing number of people who are researching and studying to know more about their history. I believe this is a wonderful and important idea, especially for those who are absent to the knowledge of their beautiful rooted history. I have also come to realize that just as many people are not only faint about their past, but even more so about their future in many cases. Some people imagine, dream or even guess about their future destination, but when it comes to straight aim specifics, they're uncertain. As a result, you have those who are searching to find their beginning and those who are strenuously wondering about their future. Both the past and the future are key elements, which need to be embraced to some degree. However, the thing that I have found to be a most powerful element is "now." There's a truth about "now" that we must tie ourselves to that it would lead us into its glory. While the power of our past heritage is fine and our future ambitions are great, the spiritual possession that we hold now is what links the full circle together. Regardless of our past heritage, be it one of great accomplishments or average achievements, the truth that we possess now is of great power. Even when it comes to our future, we have a chance to stop guessing and know more precisely some of the steps to our journey. The great power is not one of past memories or of future visions, but is one of present spiritual empowerment and insight. The mistake that's often made is that people's past can either hinder or empower them in the wrong way. For instance, what happens when you find that your past heritage was possibly linked directly to oppression or to being oppressed. This then can often fuse the wrong element of thought, because if the first generations of our families were oppressed does that have an impact on justifying our failures now. What if the earlier generations of our families were in the position as the oppressor, does that dictate the way we treat or respect people now? These are just simple examples, but possible realities that may dwell in our past, that some may allow to dictate their present, and alter their future. I believe it's o.k. to know the story, but it's better to create your own. Whatever our past was, it doesn't have to threaten, challenge, or alter our future. There is something within us that's much greater than any bloodline or external identity factor. We hold the first breed of life, which is spirit, and when we tap into that, we will find a power that will overrule anything that we have been, as well as propel us into what we will be.

    Heritage, culture, and history are all fine, however if we use these as the only factors, be it good or bad, we limit ourselves. What was done is done, but what can be, should be. We are powerful people, holding an internal knowledge that links man to a force greater than an earthly existence. When we internally see spirit and divine purpose, no longer will the facts of the past be the display of today. For in us is a power that sees past yesterday, empowers today, and sets the stage for all the tomorrows to come. We are all linked by spirit and its power of purpose.

The Gambler

I remember a movie from some years back called, "The Gambler". I thought this movie was great, but more than the movie, I liked the theme song sang by Kenny Rogers. Based on this movie about him being a gambler, the words of the theme song said, "You got to know when to hold them, know when to fold them, know when to walk away, know when to run.... etc." I found the words of this song to be most appropriate in applying them to purpose and ourselves.

When it comes to the delicateness of purpose and the intrusiveness of other people's opinions pertaining to our purpose, we have to know when to walk away and even when to run. Probably one of the most important segments of this book is the one you're reading right now! You must know that your purpose is special, divine, and it is yours! There are people in this world that will poison that which you have been called to do, if you let them. When they approach you or you find that you have wandered into the ring of negativity, you must make a decision to protect that which is sacred. When you feel the knock of infiltration on your heart or in your spirit, make the decision to walk away or even run.

In the Bible; the book of Proverbs chapter 4 verse 23 says, "Keep thy heart with all diligence; for out of it are the issues of life." In other words, we must protect our internal territory, for within it is our purpose, which we have been called to fulfill. We must keep everything that is not empowering or supportive from that which we hear, see, and know to be true. For some of us, our vision is still in an infancy state and just like a newborn baby we can't let just anybody touch and handle our precious gift. For within us is the seed that will one day grow into a powerful manifested reality. This seed, vision, and empowerment possess the power to change our lives and the lives of others. It is very important that we are keen and watchful of that which we intake into the precious ground.

Brothers and sisters let me tell you something, there are even people in our lives that may mean well with the things they say, but we must be very careful of them also. You see, man's knowledge and intention can be good, but he often knows not the vision or the mission in which God has called us to fulfill. I often say, "that natural eyes can't understand spiritual things." It is very hard at times to resist the intended love given by those close to us, but we must understand that to listen incorrectly to one could affect the lives of hundreds or even thousands. Our natural and emotional connections often have nothing to do with our spiritual destiny. Once we have locked in on the purpose in which we have been called to fulfill, this is where we must become internally protective against external intrusion. We must begin to examine and filter "all" intake. It's o.k. to stand, love, and listen but don't gamble with your destiny. Know when to walk away and know when to run!

CHAPTER 8

THE GIFT

THAT WHICH YOU POSSESS IS A BLESSING MEANT TO BLESS.

Purpose Is Motivated Without Pay

As I began writing this particular piece on purpose, a story came to mind that was more than suitable in clarifying the title. This was a story that a friend told me about a New York City tagger, the ones who spray paint the "sometimes-beautiful" graffiti on the walls of everything. This particular tagger's story is a wonderful example in explaining how purpose is motivated.

Our story begins with a storeowner who was opening up a store in New York, but due to the overall expenses of this feat, he was unable to hire a painter to beautify the outside wall of his store. He searched for reasonable priced painters, but unfortunately they were all out of his range. One of the taggers in the neighborhood heard that the storeowner was looking for some beautification, so he went to the storeowner and asked for the job. The storeowner immediately asked the young man for references. The tagger couldn't really tell him of his free-spirited work around the city, so he decided to capture this opportunity by volunteering to do the job for free. The only condition that the tagger gave was to be given the freedom to represent the store and the community through his special artist ability. Reluctantly, the storeowner agreed and for the next several weeks the tagger worked diligently painting and covering the wall with a canvas, so that the art would be a surprise. When the wall of the store was finished, he invited the storeowner, friends, and family to see the results of his hard work. To the crowd's surprise what they saw at the unveiling was a sight to behold, a portrait of the store and the community, vivid and beautifully represented. The storeowner was so pleased that he insisted on paying him something, although the pay he was given was no comparison to the rewards he would receive. Being that the store was located on the corner of a major intersection, there were many observers who drove and walked pass the store daily. The beauty of the art stunned many of them who saw the wall. As a result, the word got around about the art and the artist, and eventually other storeowners were out viewing the wall for themselves. Surely enough the tagger received many other offers around the city and was paid generously for his work. The reality of this story, is that the tagger loved to do that which was within him so much, that he was willing to do it for free. Therefore, because of the love and motivation he had for his gift, he didn't go un-rewarded.

My question to you is, are you willing to unleash that thing which is within you; without pay, regardless of the response you may get? Are you willing to say that whether they like it or hate it, this is what I must do?

This story about the tagger was only a way of saying that our gift can honestly present opportunity for us, if we are willing to do it without knowledge of the outcome. I remember writing my first book, "A Hunger To Behold" and not being sure what would happen with it. Nevertheless, I remember spending every free moment of my time working on it, because I had to get it out of me. Like a pregnant woman, it was time for me to deliver and once I delivered, let the chips fall where they may. You see, purpose is that insane drive you have to sit up half the night or even all night, coming up with ideas of how to make the unseen visible. Purpose is sometimes the puzzling reality to its observers, of a person so driven to do something that he locks himself away with himself like a mad scientist creating a monster. Apparently, being unconcerned with any reactions, responses or reward you forget about tomorrow and locks in on today that the internal vision would become external beauty. Purpose pays it holder a hundred times over by giving him life, direction, and fulfillment. All additional pay is an added bonus.

Gifts Expose God

Let's stop for a moment and ask ourselves a most important question. What is the one thing in each of our lives that expresses God's individual gift to us? Now of course the fact that we wake up each morning is more than a vividly expressed gift within itself. But what signature seed has God sown into your life that expresses his intended power through you? Is it the way you interact with people, it is your singing, or is it the great ability you have to motivate people? Whatever it is, be it big or small, God has placed something in each of us that he specifically uses to show himself through. The funny thing is that a lot of times it has nothing to do with what we have apprehended externally. To me a gift is that internal explosion, that internal execution of movement within our souls, where we find ourselves being driven to do the most amazing things. In other words, whether we design the masterful step in our head of what's to be, or whether we begin to feel the empowerment of who we are becoming. Either way, we know it's a matter of time before those around us will begin to be blessed.

Our gifts are so real, that they can internally paint the skies of our mind with what's to be. This is the conscious activity within us that eventually begins to dictate our external drive. In fact, when God has signatured this as our gift, we will often find ourselves in the midst of those who study and struggle to master that which we, "just do."

There's even a point where we will find the on-lookers wondering where we learned such a masterful skill, or how are we able to do it so "gracefully." That becomes the optimal word, "gracefully" because if we understand gifts and purpose we know these things are spiritually empowered by God. Therefore, it is his grace that shows us, leads us, and often explains the intricate parts of how we are to do what we do. So, what many people may try to base on degrees, data, and doctrine, they will find are inappropriate pertaining to our giftedness. Simply, because what we possess is divine. I mean let's examine a little closer the truth at hand; there are many people who study how to play the piano for years. They read and study the history, they study the composition of pianos, and they even hire known teachers of the art. Nevertheless, many still fall short of putting any major melody to flight or should I say, any truly recognized melody to flight. Meanwhile you will find some kid who has too much time on his hand, somewhere tapping away on his church piano or maybe on the little keyboard that his parents bought him for Christmas. Now at first, fear or uncertainty is what divides him and this technical instrument. However, after many strokes of curiosity, some thing clicks within and he realizes that he understands what he hears. He realizes there is something within that's catching the notes so deeply that he not only hears them, but he feels them. He and the music become one in existence; for the music speaks to him, and through the music he speaks. Amazingly, these are the very people that sit under the lights of accomplishment and win our hearts. Evidence such as this can be rare, but it happens, and it happens for those who give way to their gift.

I have found that at times, we amaze even ourselves by our ability to do, that which is within. Our gift becomes more than just a talent; it becomes an empowerment. Situations like the boy and the piano causes the world to notice the greater force. They recognize the force of pure internal ability and power, as well as the force of giftedness. In addition, they are somewhat exposed to the creator and motivator of this awesome force, which is God. I have seen little boys from the ghetto with nothing, sore to become great figures in our very sight. I have seen the outcasted, the unlearned, and the nobodies of yesterday; become the gifted somebodies of today. I have seen God... in the midst!

Another Life Form

More frequently these days it seems that many people are wondering, "is this great and seemingly infinite universe limited to just us?" To be more direct the question that's being asked "is there life on other planets?" We have gotten so thirsty for the fulfillment to these questions that a chosen few have even said to have seen our universal neighbors and their foreign vehicles. In an arena where many have never seen for themselves, most hold more to an internal belief than anything else. Some of us feel the empowerment to believe in the existence of universal life as we reach to grasp a greater understanding of life and our existence. Other life forms are just one avenue which man has chosen to travel in an attempt to get that heightened level of understanding and completeness; as many of us remain bound here on earth. You will notice, even in our music, movies and scientific deliveries that we try to teach and tell the world of a great or greater reality than the one we embrace within our daily walk. However, my question becomes, "is the connection that we feel really that of a greater physical life existence from beyond or is that the most tangibly accepted explanation?" I do believe that other life forms exist, possible beyond our travel capabilities. But most importantly, I believe that wherever there is other life existence, they too could feel the same pull of a greater existence as well. My next question therefore will be, "did our Creator mean for us to spend our time dabbling in the curiosity of what exists elsewhere or should our search be to discover the unexplored territory and power that lies within?" Could it be that the pull we feel exist not outward and away, but rather inward and near?" The pull and belief of a distant life form could be that thus far, we have lived within mere natural limitations, failing to really explore the spiritual ground within. Think about it, when we understand that we and all else that exists are part of He who created us; the Creator. Then, we understand that the pull could be to help us unlock our spiritual identity and purpose, that which is seeking to be freed. To clearly explain it, if we were to find another life form; probably outside of some physical or as some believe, mental advantage they probably share that same pull of a higher central source of existence.

I truly believe that once we look inward and explore spirit and purpose, then we shall find the true greater life form. With so much power within, the question is not what's out there, but more so why are "we" here? What was God's plan for putting us here? What did he want accomplished? Did he give us a beginning, hoping that as we grew and discovered true spiritual existence and purpose, that it would lead us truly back to Him? I believe that there could be other life forms out there that have possibly reached the point whereby they too are being pulled to recognize a greater existence, but like us they also have possibly failed to look within. The truth is not always found externally in what we see, but powerfully in what we internally are being led to discover. If you examine this chapter carefully, it is designed to teach us about purpose. It's to help us see that our purpose lies not in the connection of discovering a greater external existence, but more so in the discovery of a great internal truth and power that awaits. We may not see a

Starving to Live

new world billions of miles away, but we can see and help to present a new world that exist right within us. Each of our purposes is part of the overall purpose to help heighten our existence in how we exist. There is a life waiting to be discovered when we seek to find our existence within. Let the drive of belief carry us to purpose, that it would expose within us, "another life form."

CHAPTER 9

FIRE FUELS THE FIERCE!

THERE ARE MANY ELEMENTS THAT WILL EMPOWER THAT WHICH YOU ARE CALLED TO DO.

Vitamins For Purpose

I know some may find it hard to believe, but there are vitamins for purpose. These are not vitamins that you put in your mouth, but vitamins that you put in your heart. They do nothing for the body, but they do wonders for the mind. Purpose vitamins are those daily doses of nutrients, which cause us to grow inward. These vitamins enrich, enhance and empower the purpose within us. They can play a powerful part in strengthening the reality of our ability to fulfill and achieve our purpose. They also have the ability to empower the unseen, helping to transform belief into reality and unfulfillment into fulfillment.

I remember, I started consciously taking these vitamins everyday around about the time I turned 35 years old. The reason was I had reached a point in my life that something had to happen. I knew I had a purpose, but I wasn't sure how to get to it, or how to nurture it and allow it to nurture me. Right about that same time, I recall becoming very intrigued with biographies and documentaries. I started off reading biblical stories on the lives of great men like Jesus, Moses, David, Joseph, and others. I also read bits and pieces on Martin Luther King, Malcolm X, Booker T. Washington, Muhammad Ali, and Marcus Garvey. I became hungry to find out how these people became who they were. What was it that they discovered, that unlocked their great destinies? I realized that they all started out as just ordinary people like anyone else. However, at some point these men came to the crossing where they met purpose and their lives were changed. This made me even hungrier, unfortunately because I hung on to every word that I read, it often took me weeks or months to read some books. Then I began to notice biographies on television about actors, athletes and singers such as Michael Jackson, Michael Jordan, The Temptations, Sammy Davis Jr. and others. I digested as much as possible, not realizing what these vitamins were doing to me. They were empowering me to know that the extraordinary were the ordinary, until they grabbed hold to their purpose. Best of all, they let purpose lead them onto the stage of fulfillment, in spite of the obstacles or setbacks they faced. It got to the point that I wanted to hear anything that told the story of people like me, who reached to fulfill their purpose. Daily I would be starving to find food; be it stories on writers, artists, even business stories of entrepreneurs. Suddenly, these daily vitamins began to fuel the fire in the belief of my purpose and achievement. They showed me that the inward seed could explode into outward reality. It revealed how the ordinary and average could grab hold to purpose and become the gifted and extraordinary. The funny thing is, it wasn't necessarily just about money and fame, but more so about releasing and fulfilling purpose, that which we think about and dream about. Purpose, that living light which burns deep within our souls; crying for life.

 I'm telling you, on those days when I felt doubtful or frustrated, I would grab my bible or search the channels to find vitamins. I periodically even found myself at the bookstore reading the autobiographies of various writers. To put it plain and simple, I needed my vitamins. I needed to be constantly reminded that achievement was possible and purpose was powerful. I needed to know that the start didn't

Starving to Live

always dictate the finish. I needed to find anyone like myself, who became empowered with purpose and allow it to lead them to their destiny. These became my daily vitamins in which I insisted on taking. Whatever it is that you believe or desire to do, find the vitamins that are just right for you; whether its scriptures, songs, books or television shows, and let them help to empower your belief into reality.

Fury!

Are you mad? Good! Are you furious? Great. Because, it's not until we get mad enough that we sometimes decide to do something about that which frustrates us. One of the most important points about the power of fury is correctly aiming it and letting it go. I truly believe that if it's tunneled through our gift, it can cause an explosion of pure and intense energy. When truth and purpose are brewing on the inside to the point that they're causing disorder in our lives, that's the mark that truth can no longer be suppressed or ignored. Unlike some people, who often override this reality by reason of fear, money, or pressure, we know that we must release this internal fire and do exactly what we were designed to do. We hear the calling and we feel the reality of that which is within, telling us that the volcano is about to erupt. It kind of reminds me of one of those tropical island movies, where the islanders sing and dance to calm the volcano. Nevertheless, with all of their singing and dancing, though the volcano appears cool and calm on the outside, brewing beneath the ground is a gargantuan abyss of hot liquid anger that eventually screams. In the same manner, for some who are reading this book right now, your blood is brewing, your heart is pounding and the fury is starting to surface. You've tried to live your life ordinary, routine, and comfortable, but this internal fury is demanding attention. And to make one point clear, by no means are we going to snap our finger and "presto", our needs and support system appears. But while we wait, we should research, pray, or whatever we need to do, to help us arrive at our destination. We need to take this internal fury and make it speak, in the sense of letting it be the edge for whatever it is that we desire to do. If it's singing, then let it be the passion that infuses our song. If it's painting, then let it be the force that guides each stroke. Whatever it is, let this fury empower your vision and take you to the edge, beyond the norm. Don't be afraid to let people hear your passion, your power, and your fury through whatever it is that you desire to do.

I recall my grandmother loving to cook, and I noticed that she never used a recipe book. One day I asked her, how did she know how to prepare such great dishes? She told me, "Son it's within me, my passion for cooking is in me, it's what I do." Now I have had some of the same dishes she cooked, prepared around the country, either at restaurants or while visiting with various people. Let me tell you something, no matter what recipe they followed, nor who the restaurants had working in the kitchen, none of it tasted as great as some of grandmother's cooking. If you are wondering how this connects with what we're talking about, let me make it a little simpler. When grandmother was happy, she cooked. When grandmother was upset with my grandfather, she cooked. When grandmother had that something on her mind that only her and God could talk about, she cooked. My grandmother's ability to put life into food was fused by what was within. Simple story, powerful point.

I know right now some of you are frustrated or upset because you are stuck in a rut and can't seem to get anyone to answer the door that you have been knocking on. Well, what I am telling you is to channel that energy into your gift and blast that door down.

Take for an instance rap music, which I am no stranger to, some I like and some I don't. If the truth be told, one of the reasons some rap is so successful is that some of these young messengers are writing from fury. Not anger, but from the energy of fury. It's like being born with something to say and never really being sure if you are going to get the chance to be heard. So, what they do is scream in the wind. In other words, they write as if someone is listening, and in the event that the wind does carry their message, whoever's ears it hit, it stuns. Sometimes good and sometimes bad, either way it stuns. I believe everybody has a following, from the politically correct to the rudest of the gifted. My point is, if they're out there waiting and your day is to come, then when you deliver your gift make it a shot to the heart. Let it be as precisely desired, as morphine is for pain. I truly believe that the empowerment of fury is like the unseen drive that makes a kid that's been bullied, one day launch back on that bully and fight him with no consideration of the outcome. Fury, when harnessed to and through our purpose often becomes the factor which gives our inner voice range and power. Fury; the fire, the fuel, the force!

Sorrow

A lot of the topics in this book have been titled with clever and quaint names. This was done to introduce the topic in such a way that you would be curious to know what exactly was in the context beyond that title. Unlike many of the other topics, this topic was titled according to what it will actually speak about; "sorrow."

If you ask almost anyone about sorrow, you will find that this is an issue that has periodically plagued all of our lives. It seems literally from the moment we became of a conscious age, in which we began to venture out into the world, sorrow was one of the greeters that gave great introduction. It would almost seem needless to say that sorrow is something that with great effort, we try to avoid. Like trying to avoid seeing the sun some days, unless we are going to stay in the house, it is impossible. If that would be our strategy to stay in the house, it's amazing how the sun can seep through even the smallest crack.

In a book that has been written to give understanding and help in empowering purpose, I was almost apprehensive to include this segment. However, I have come to realize that in this day and time we must not blindly walk through life, not even when it comes to purpose. As the maturity and power in me stirs, I must be honest with those who embrace this book. It is my mission to tell you not only of the days of purpose, but of the nights also. Though the topic of sorrow may appear to be intrusive and invading to the ears, it must be understood for maturity sake.

There are elements that we face in life at various times, call them what you may; struggles, suffering, challenges, or simply the weights of life. I find that the word sorrow often describes the result of these realities. When we drive along the road of life and reach the stormy areas of sorrow we are faced with choices. Do we pull over and wait for the storm to pass or do we press on to our destination? When sorrow comes it brings our journey of travel to a screeching halt, if we let it. Sorrow can make us pull over or even head in the other direction, away from our appointed destinations. Although we don't look for sorrow it can exist in various places along our journey. I truly believe that sorrow like any other challenging element in life, has a purpose as well. Most importantly, I believe it is a filtering tool that allows only the fine to pass through, those who are true to their belief. It can be the defining and refining element that can shape and challenge who we are to become. The blade of sorrow can cut to the core of who we really are, exposing this truth to others and ourselves. Sorrow is not welcomed in our lives, but when it comes and goes we find that it has added depth to our character. It gives volume to our voice and validity to our knowledge. Sorrow is the pain that chokes us or forces us to breathe. It forces us to make the decision to live and live fiercely, or die beaten. Sorrow can force us to see certain realities and make changes, which can often lead us into our purpose. It can be the tool that breaks the stone, exposing the diamond. There are so many people who I believe had what it took to beautifully etch their mark in this world. However, I believe sorrow met these people along their journey; stared them in their eyes, breathed in their face, called their bluff and eventually forced them to turn back. In these cases where we are confronted by sorrow along our journey, we must turn the table on it, so that it becomes our springboard. As a result of its force trying to push us to the bottom of the sea, we must let the resistance of our determined "will" persevere, to force us back up.

I further believe that in life when we stand face to face with people, there is a great factor that validates us. This factor is not often found merely in the words that we speak, but in the evidence of our eyes from preserving through sorrow. This becomes the evidence that often validates our journey and us. In other words, it's not what we say, but often what we have lived. I hope you have accepted and maybe even appreciated the need for this intended message of help. For if sorrow is not understood in a full perspective, it will be remembered as the demise of who we could have been.

The Wind

The wind represents the brisk realities that we feel daily as we stand outside of purpose. It's the chilling reality that blows morning, noon, and night letting us know that we are alive externally, while possibly dying internally. Often times we try to block out the wind with the windows of our mind, overriding it; acting as if it doesn't exist. However, the wind can creep up into our souls and push the smell of purpose right into our nostrils, making us breathe its powerful reality. As a result, we often rush to the refuge of our jobs in hope that our job will shield us from this force. Fortunately, yes I said fortunately, the wind is too powerful of a reality for even the walls of jobs to shield. The wind is the cold reality that blows from a hollow soul of unfulfilled purpose. The wind can bring tears to our eyes as we sometimes stand face to face in it. It can cut to shreds the thin garment of accepted mediocrity and blow open the coat of complacency. The wind can blow deeply enough to reach the bare nakedness of our heart to remind and warn us that something is dying. The wind's total purpose is to consciously lift us to the point, that we are driven to reach our destination. We shouldn't fight it, hide from it, or try to avoid it. We should rather embrace the wind that it would blow life into us and lead us to the place of purpose as we are pushed towards its fulfillment.

For some of us, we have grown comfortable within the walls of justification; be it failures or external accomplishments. We refuse to come out from behind the barriers of an average content life, so there we stay in hope that the wind of reality will eventually go away. Although at times it may die down and even momentarily seem to stop, it will eventually pick back up and once again blow with great intensity. It's good that we have the wind, because on many days we walk through life too comfortable. The wind serves as a reminder that there is something much greater that we should be doing. In fact, the more we dwell outside of purpose the more brisk the wind becomes. In the literal sense of the wind, it is amazing how it seems to find the slightest opening in our garments, to seep in and make its presence known. I truly believe that when purpose is fulfilled, that very same wind will becomes the refreshing breeze of reality that reminds us of our fulfilled purpose.

CHAPTER 10

LOSE YOURSELF!

YOU MUST FORGET ABOUT PAST FAILURES, PRESENT OBSTACLES, AND FUTURE FEARS, AND LOSE YOURSELF IN THAT WHICH YOU ARE PURPOSED TO DO.

You're Adding The Wrong Numbers

Purpose is powerful for numerous reasons. First purpose is often times unassociated with our external strengths and weaknesses. We may be talented or lack talent externally, just to find out that there is something greater within us that defines who we shall become. The funny thing about purpose is it can be buried so deeply within us, that it's not until mid-way through our lives, as we attempt to gain greater fulfillment that purpose is revealed.

I often think about how parents tell their children that based on their present actions, they are going to amount to very little or nothing. Some of those same children later in age reached a defining moment, be it hardship or other motivations that pushed them to dig and succeed through the apprehension of purpose. All of us have to find ourselves by addition and subtraction, experiment, and exploration. As a result, at some point we come to the realization, that maybe we've been wandering down the wrong road or have been reading the wrong maps in search of fulfillment. Whenever and however this happens, we will find that often, all of us at one time or another have added the wrong numbers in the equation of our final outcome. We have been associating where we've been with where we're going, and who we were with who we believe we can be.

Most importantly, we have accepted the equation of how other people view us instead of what's on the inside of us, which is the true determining factor of who we shall become. I'm telling you my friends, don't let the negative equations of anyone, including self, be the final equation for your life. There is something great within all of us, which can take the low numbers of who we are and with the great multiplying power of purpose, sum up unlimited potential towards who we shall be. For if you add one man, plus purpose, with nothing to lose, and faith in God, it will equal "one" magnificent power in motion. The fact of the matter is that those who are known today were the unknowns of yesterday and those who are unknown of today will be the known of tomorrow. Got it? Good!

Free!

In the fall of 2002, I had the opportunity to partake in African American History class. I was blessed to learn a lot about my ancestors and the struggles they faced as slaves here in America. One of the things that really stuck out to me was the mental strength many of them possessed, while they lived trapped in the reality of two worlds. The first reality was that they would be forever haunted by the vivid reality of their kidnapped freedom and their murdered honor, which they now held only in memory. I believe that they would be punished continuously by the detail images of their beautiful homeland. There the trees stretched endlessly to the night sky, as to welcome God's presence upon the earth. In addition, I believe they could still hear within the wind, the songs of their ancestors as it blew through the night carrying the message of faith and hope. They knew with great reality who and what they were. They were powerful people, descendants of kings and queens. But, within a devastating moment their honor, dignity, and freedom was taken. Can you imagine the reality of knowing internally the power you possess, while all along being enslaved and oppressed in a system totally foreign to everything that you know as living? Most of all, can you imagine the agony of internally knowing who you are, your designed destiny, versus who you are now forced to be? How do you live a life that's false in every aspect of how God designed it to be? How do you live though each waking day in a reality such as this? How do you live chained and bound, while the smell of greatness lingers in your nose? I truly believe that greater than the physical agony they faced, many of them had to face an even greater internal reality. As an African poet so powerfully put it, "my bruises are a hard dark reminder of my past, but the internal reality of who I should be, is a constant blinding light of my present."

Now, in no way can we compare any of our suffering to the agony in which my great ancestor suffered; in no way mistake that. In a very small way though, I use this illustration to symbolize the pain that is felt when you live or have been forced to live in any other reality other than the one you were created to live. By whatever means, some of us have come face to face with the reality that we are greater than who we have thus far accepted to be. In fact, we soulfully know that we are meant to be free. We can smell the aroma of power churning within, but daily we fearfully face and accept the reality of an oppressed life. Many of my ancestors died because in no way could they accept a life of slavery as an alternative. Whether it meant dying while trying to escape or a self inflicted death, slavery was not acceptable. For many of them to live anything other than free in mind, body, and soul was already a death in itself. So I challenge you, for there's no one holding you back, escape from what you have been forced to do and live free in what you are destined to do. Some may say this was an extreme to use such an illustration. I say to you, whoever you are, regardless of your race, color or your past, if it takes this shared reality to make you embrace your destiny, then so be it. I leave this thought with you, "to live any way other than free, is to do everything other than to live." Escape now! For fulfillment awaits!

The Force

Can you feel it or are you acting as if it's not there? You know, that annoying racing energy within us, that's demanding that we leap out of the boat of complacency and into the rapids of our true destiny. Yeah, I know it doesn't seem to make sense as this fierce reality rumbles within us like a raging fall on a windy day. I also know it's hard to even explain what we feel; if we could, who do we tell of this current of power flowing within us? How do we explain this reality, which at times it seems as if it's going to lift us up off our feet? We've tried to mentally contain it and even ignore it, but it won't be denied. We even periodically find ourselves talking to it, as we question the intent and realism of its presence. How did this nagging internal energy come to be, and why won't it accept our present position in life? Why does it seem to demand of us the seemingly impossible? In fact, its power, its reality, and its foresight are contradictory to the present external measurement of who we are. So then, why is this force so real within us?

First, as I have continuously explained, we must realize that God has given each of us a mission and a destination. However, some of us have veered off the predestined course to seek other chosen treasures. But, at some point we run head on into something that triggers the eruption of this hidden force. The triggering mechanism can be timing, as it cracks the seal releasing purpose into our lives or maybe it's the altitude of reached maturity. Perhaps it's the weighted pressure of an unfulfilled life that causes it to burst into reality. Whatever way it happens, baby believe me-it's real! The force is so intrusive that it cares less where we are in life, what we are doing or who we are with. I say again, it cares not who we are with; for it accepts not the justifications of us being married, having children or the fact of people counting on us at our present status. Now don't be mistaken, I am not trying to say that these factors are irrelevant, but if we are not careful, they can become excuses. Due to the fact, that the world is full of married, committed, fathers and mothers who even in entering the golden years of their lives, met purpose and took flight. It is my belief, that even if one of these reasons does fit your particular life, that there's still unimaginable power and fulfillment that can be brought to your life as you change from a mild mannered reporter into super.....! Only you know what it is that's burning within you, that's screaming to become the identity of who you really are. However, until you accept the truth of the greater calling and higher purpose, your life will never be complete. In fact, only you know the feeling of lying awake in bed at night envisioning what you could become. Only you know the feeling of seeing someone else living his or her dream or doing that which you desire to do. How long will you accept this as just an annoying feeling or a daydreamer's energy? You must grab hold to the force; that undeniable hunger, that fierce wind and let it lead you into freedom. You must let it surface into an accepted reality and watch as it overwhelms you and those around you with life, as it takes you beyond the shores of the shallow-into the deep! The force is real, it's pure; it's that deeply seeded, un-tampered reality of who we were meant to be. It's that which brings tears to our eyes, knots in our throat, and butterflies in our stomach when we think about it. Why you ask, because it lives! As so dramatically spoken in the movie Star Wars, "you must let the force guide you Luke." I know you thought I was going to say, "may the force be with you," but the truth of the matter is, it's already there. You know it and I know it. Be true to the truth.

The Boxer and The Fighter

I once heard a great boxer say, "Sometimes a fight is not won by skill or by talent, nor by the efforts of training, but rather on fight night who has the greatest will to win." I have seen some of the greatest boxers get knocked out by "unknown-untitled nobodies" and shock the world. If we had only looked into the eyes of these so called "nobodies," we wouldn't have been surprised. I believe that what sometimes gives a fighter the edge over a boxer, is his will, his drive, and his hunger for victory. A boxer can be a skilled technician, a master executioner of offense and defense. He can love the sport and understand it to the fullest. He can master the angles, develop split second response and even control his breathing. As a result, all of these things make him a fine tuned machine, with all parts working in unison. On the other hand, you have the fighter; lets say one unknown in the public eye. For him fighting is what he breathes; his fists are his chosen weapons of choice on his day-to-day battleground. His senses are more of a paranoid cautiousness, than a defense. He attacks to keep from being attacked. He fights to end each war without retaliation. His trainer sees the fire, the fury, and the force; he therefore chooses to alter the rawness of this fighter as little as possible, only making him appropriately knowledgeable for each fight. With basic assistance as far as training, this fighter gets the opportunity of a lifetime to not only gain a belt and wealth, but also respect and recognition for, "who and what he is."

It's fight night, the fighter and the boxer enter the ring, and they stand toe to toe. Between the two, the boxer appears more confident as a result of all of his accomplishments, the applause and the hype. Meanwhile, the fighter examines his opponent, staring deeply into his eyes; seeking to detect any weakness. They return to their corners, the bell rings, they come out, the boxer bobs and weaves, they meet and with everything within his soul the fighter throws his first punch. The fighter blasts the boxer's guard slightly to the side, catching a fraction of his chin, Stop!

Now, what has just happened within this second is that the boxer realizes from the force of the fighter's single assault, that this is not a boxing match, but a fight. He also realizes from that same felt force, that his opponent the fighter does not have a polished technique. In fact, he realizes that the fighter's only objective is to fight; win or lose, the fighter is there to fight. In a broad sense of the word fight means to engage in combat with an objective to defeat and overthrow. From the angle of the fighter, to fight is not a thing of science and mathematics, belts and money, but it is a thing of survival. This is the only reality that some of us have; that we must and will survive! We are challenged and threatened by life, but we triumph. Most Importantly, for some of us, our survival and our refusal to non-exist is the only thing that tells us who we are and that we're still alive. Therefore, no opponent who has simply practiced a skill will stand toe to toe with us and overcome the soulful force, "that is us."

Now, we resume back to the fight. With the first punch not only has the boxer's guard been slightly penetrated, but also a truth has been internally declared. For the boxer realizes that his opponent has won by reason and that reason is,

Starving to Live

he has no excuse not to fight. For he is operating "in" the pure, uninterrupted power of who he is, "a true unstoppable force." The next punch catches everything; guard, chin, jaw, the works, sending the boxer to the canvas and with a ten count the fight is over. At the end of the fight during the interview, the reporter asked the fighter, "what was your game plan", and the fighter simply said, "to unleash my identity."

Now, this story could be debatable, but what's not debatable is who we are internally, up and coming champions. We're not trying to knockout the successful boxers, who exist within the ring of life, but the fact of the matter is, though they may have gained recognition for their accomplishments, some of them and I did say "some" couldn't stand toe to toe with us. Because, what some may do for whatever reason; be it skillfulness, timing, association or being in the right place at the right time, for us it's the pure identity of who we are. Even when we train, it's more so a bout against ourselves, to defeat our known weaknesses. We are what we are and we do what we do; that which we do is our soulful right, it's our identity. So while we sit ringside in admiration of some boxers, the only true difference between them and us is "action." Above all, right this minute someone holds a title that could be rightfully ours. Those knots in our stomach, those tears in our eyes, those internal reactions that we get whenever we hear a bell ring is only trying to tell us, "it's fight time!" We were not made to sit by the ring; we were design to be in the ring!

The Fear Factor

When it comes to life and purpose, are we playing it safe or are we simply halted by fear? In many cases we walk through life, so called playing it safe, staying on logically sound ground, living strictly where we can see the certainties of life. Playing it safe protects us from embarrassment, exposure, and rejection. "Safe" is a place that keeps our rational and logical supporters happy. "Safe" is all the explainable elements in our life which help to justify soundness in what we are typically suppose to be. It's the unspoken standard, in which the norm is measured by. In fact, anything beyond those measurements can be defined as foolish or careless.

The question that must be posed however, is safe an empowerment or a poison for purpose. It is my belief, that playing it safe is what sometimes supports mediocrity. Playing it safe kills our hunger and ability to fulfill purpose, which in some cases could lead to greatness. In an unwelcomed reality, safe is the unfaced truth of existing fear, especially if we know that we have been called "to the great beyond", metaphorically speaking, from which we stand. While this calling and empowerment loudly echoes within our souls, we continuously measure and examine our present state of existence. As a result, fear then magnifies the reality of risking our accomplished position. Fear illuminates both the reality of where we are and questions the belief of where we believe we are destined to go. Fear causes us to close our eyes to what we think is the uncertain, while all along internally we are certain. When we close our eyes, we can't see our steps and when we can't see our steps, we refuse to move. As a result of refusing to move, we fearfully justify our position as "safe." Fear helps to devise a list of sound factors, which stand in opposition to that which we are told to be unsound. Fear dictates our movement, it questions anything beyond what we safely know and see. Fear can cause a ship destined to sail the seven seas, to never leave the dock. Unfortunately, while the ship is admired by other smaller docked boats, it never reaches the legendary status of other voyagers of its kind. Fear regulates our acceptance and response. It tells us what is acceptable and what we should believe and respond to. This is based on the programmed measurements of the norm and sometimes majority. The "fear factor" can't kill purpose however; it can help to maintain separation long enough that we miss our window of opportunity to fulfill purpose.

It is most important that we wake up and recognize that fear is the factor that we too often embrace, which keeps us safe in a so called, "safe place." The only fear factor that we should focus on is the fact that because of our safe position, we may cease to execute the actions, which will truly define and determine who we are meant to be. Whether safely behind fear or fearfully behind safe, either way we may cease to exist.

Be Encouraged

On my most fearful day, I could not cease from doing that which I was internally led to achieve. Keeping my eyes on the internal prize was sometimes challenged by great external distractions. Fortunately, one of the great realizations that I came to was that my purpose was bigger than just me. As easy as it seemed to sometimes possibly take another route, I realized that there was a calling in which I had to fulfill. My purpose in a seemingly crazy way was overpowering at times, as if it had hold of me and was not going to let me go. There was an internal reality that was in no way being influenced externally. Though it may have been externally confirmed every now and then, what I knew to be true was all of an internal assurance. This truth was often exposed through meditation and even sometimes isolation. I knew there was something great and powerful stirring within, just like I believe many of you know. But unfortunately, I kept searching and waiting for externally validation. The reason being, it's sometimes easier to understand what we see, more often than what we feel.

More importantly for some of us, it's easier to justify that which is externally acceptable. When we look around, most people seem to be following to some degree, the pattern of the norm. They take on that which is comfortable and which make sense to themselves and those around them. This pre-paved pattern presents no risk and little to no judgment. Unfortunately, many will one day look back and possibly discover that the true power and reward was in that which "seemed" to be a risk. For those of us who internally are "starving to live", we cannot afford not to take this divine stance. Like a person searching to find a loved one who they once knew, sometimes the only thing that we hold is the internal image that drives us. Truthfully, if you have ever been deeply touched internally, you know that the journey must be taken. What may seem to be crazy to those who stand in judgment becomes a beacon of light to us, even when we close our eyes. We were not placed here on this earth by chance to wander aimlessly, but rather placed here to purposely exist.

There is a saying, "what you don't know can't hurt you." I believe this saying to be true. For what you don't know can't hurt you, it can "kill you" if you are not careful. The you that I am speaking of is the internal you, which waits in anticipation to live out it's purpose. The false image of a pre-paved life is acceptable for most, but I feel that it is a great dishonor to our Creator. It's like receiving a gift wrapped in a beautiful box, and in amazement of the wrapping, you never look inside the box to see the gift itself.

Purpose can be a scary thing because it cries, tugs and challenges us to see and walk initially in the deepness of the uncertain. I have heard fishermen say, that the most treasured fishing spots are the places where the water is very deep and the average person is too afraid to go. In a similar manner, I believe that deep within each of us are uncharted areas that possess great treasures to be obtained. However, fear keeps us in the safe and shallow waters of existence. When you do finally discover within yourself that place of power, freedom and fulfillment, light the trail that others may journey to find the reward of fulfillment as well. Don't starve to live, live to feed. Be encouraged, for your purpose is powerful!

Conclusion to the Matter

It is sad to think of the many people who have died or will die, and never fulfill their purpose. Though this book was written in an attempt to help you to understand your purpose, it could never replace the "Purpose giver."

Jesus said in St. John chapter 14 verse 6, "I am the way, the truth, and the life: no man cometh unto the Father, but by me." It is at this time that I would like to extend an invitation to you to come to know the Father, the giver of all purposes, through Jesus Christ. Until you accept Christ in your life, you can never "truly" know your purpose, or how to properly execute it.

Is your life and purpose worth coming to know Christ? If so, then sincerely ask Jesus to forgive you for all your sins, and then ask him to come into your heart and be Lord over your life. Ask him to make his purpose and direction for your life known. Finally, thank Jesus for what he has done, and will do in your life.